Risk management and failure

# Praise for *Too Good To Fail?*

'This is an honest to goodness book written by an honest to goodness manager. Rich in detail and experiences; essential reading. There is a lesson on every page, a message in every paragraph and an example on every line. I loved it.'

**Roy Lilley, former NHS Trust Chair, writer and broadcaster**

*'Too Good to Fail?* is that rare thing: a combination of general principles and concrete advice which is of equal relevance to public and private sectors. It is a book to be used and treasured, and one that I wholeheartedly recommend.'

**Professor Alison Wolf, CBE, Sir Roy Griffiths Professor of Public Sector Management, King's College London**

'Every manager can learn from this very readable book as they walk the tightrope between success and failure.

Jan Filochowski has drawn on a fascinating career in the health sector to give us some footholds for the climb to the top – complete with memorable case studies and personal wisdom.

This book is a must for anyone interested in improving their management skills - it makes for great learning and great reading.'

**Chris Green, ex Chief Executive, Virgin Trains**

'A very wise and reflective book on one of the toughest management tasks of all – recovering from failure – by one of the most experienced turnaround CEOs in the NHS. Valuable lessons for every senior manager in every organisation.'

**Professor Daniel T. Jones, author of *The Machine that Changed the World* and *Lean Thinking***

# Too Good to Fail?

# Too Good
# to Fail?

How management gets
it wrong and how you
can get it right

**Jan Filochowski**

**PEARSON**

Harlow, England • London • New York • Boston • San Francisco • Toronto • Sydney
Auckland • Singapore • Hong Kong • Tokyo • Seoul • Taipei • New Delhi
Cape Town • São Paulo • Mexico City • Madrid • Amsterdam • Munich • Paris • Milan

**PEARSON EDUCATION LIMITED**

Edinburgh Gate
Harlow CM20 2JE
United Kingdom
Tel: +44 (0)1279 623623
Web: www.pearson.com/uk

**First published 2013** (print and electronic)

ISBN: 978-0-273-78523-1 (print)
      978-0-273-78863-8 (PDF)
      978-0-273-78862-1 (ePub)

*British Library Cataloguing-in-Publication Data*
A catalogue record for the print edition is available from the British Library

*Library of Congress Cataloging-in-Publication Data*
Filochowski, Jan.
  Too good to fail? : how management gets it wrong and how you can get it right / Jan Filochowski.
    pages cm.
  Includes index.
  ISBN 978-0-273-78523-1 (pbk.)
  1. Management. 2. Decision making. 3. Problem solving. 4. Business faillures. 5. Success in business. I. Title.
  HD31.F5143 2013
  658--dc23
                        2013011274

**The Financial Times**. With a worldwide network of highly respected journalists, the *Financial Times* provides global business news, insightful opinion and expert analysis of business, finance and politics. With over 500 journalists reporting from 50 countries worldwide, our in-depth coverage of international news is objectively reported and analysed from an independent, global perspective. To find out more, visit www.ft.com/pearsonoffer.

10 9 8 7 6 5 4 3 2 1

17 16 15 14 13

Cover design by Dan Mogford
Print edition typeset in 10.25/14pt Frutiger LT Pro by 30
Print edition printed and bound in Great Britain by Henry Ling at the Dorset Press, Dorchester, Dorset

NOTE THAT ANY PAGE CROSS-REFERENCES REFER TO THE PRINT EDITION

# Contents

# About the author

Jan Filochowski is currently Chief Executive of the world famous Great Ormond Street Hospital for Children. He was educated at Cambridge, Newcastle, Oxford and Harvard Universities. He has spent his 37 year career working in healthcare, and during the last 20 years has been a CEO of six different hospital and healthcare organisations and become widely known as a successful turnaround specialist for his work in some of them. He was named as one of the three heroes of the NHS in 2003 by the *Health Service Journal*, who described him as a serial improver of failing hospitals. He has also acted as an adviser to a number of organisations, including the Department of Health and the Prime Minister's Delivery Unit. Jan has been a Visiting Professor in the Department of Information Systems at Brunel University since 2004.

# Acknowledgements

The origins of this book go back nearly 10 years. In that time many, many people have helped me with it. I would like to express my appreciation to the following in particular: Steve Collins, sadly no longer with us, for suggesting shortly after I had moved on from the Royal United Hospital in Bath in 2003 that I put my findings and ideas about failure and recovery into an article; Nick Edwards and Alaistair McLelland, at the *Health Service Journal*, for asking me and helping me to do more and create a series of articles, and for publishing them; Bob Fryer, then head of the NHS University, who when he saw the articles said they were good but a job half done, leading to the NHS University awarding me a Fellowship to turn the ideas into a book; to Wolfson College and the Judge Institute at Cambridge University for hosting me for that Fellowship year (2004–5); to Nick Brearley for astutely pointing out what was missing from my ideas before declining to publish me; to Professor Alison Wolf of King's College and Professor Terry Young of Brunel University for their detailed and deeply helpful comments; to Sally Holloway, my agent, who guided me and pushed me to make the book more coherent and accessible and helped me find the right publisher; to Gail Samuel, my PA at West Hertfordshire Hospitals who gave huge amounts of her own time and her boundless energy typing up redraft after redraft and transforming the book's presentation; and, lastly and most importantly, my wife, Naomi, who has consistently, throughout the book's gestation, been a most insightful and sympathetic reviewer, and has constantly supported and encouraged me, notably at the times when I got really discouraged and might have given up. Naturally, the book's faults remain mine.

## PUBLISHER'S ACKNOWLEDGEMENTS

The publisher wishes to thank Roy Lilley for permission to use an extract from his blog on pages 46–7.

In some cases we have been unable to trace the owners of copyright material, and we would appreciate any information that would enable us to do so.

# Foreword

When I first met Jan, he had already spent his year at Harvard and was starting to enjoy success at Medway. He came across as a thoughtful, confident, problem solver with time to tease away the obvious and an interest in the profound. I particularly liked his appetite for taking abstract concepts and turning them into workable process.

So when I first saw the sketch of a rocky cavern, descending into the darker realms of failure before climbing the far bank into operational sunshine, I felt Jan was onto something. I was taken by the distinction he drew between the underlying state of an organisation and the way in which it was perceived – even by those inside it. I found his narrative insightful and his illustrations lent credence to it. And now, a dozen or more years since we first met, Jan's track record has justified the promise: he has applied his ideas sufficiently often to lay claim to having a system, and he has enjoyed enough success to claim that it works.

Although Lean Thinking has made its mark on Jan, you will not find an ideological commitment to Lean, or indeed, to any other of the manufacturing philosophies that have proven popular with theorists of late. Rather, you will encounter a pragmatic approach that blends to taste and morphs around the problems. By presenting a framework of ideas, Jan encourages you to join in and think your way through. For me, the practicality is the heart of the attraction of this book, and the combination of an accessible framework with the eclectic illustrations makes this book well worth the read.

We have stayed in touch over the years and I have enjoyed seeing these concepts hit the public domain through a set of articles in the *Health Service Journal*. Some of the ideas we discussed when first we met – such as problem-knowledge couplers – are not as prominent as they once were in putting the story together. Some things have assumed much greater importance: the more mundane business, for instance, of drawing the right pictures to influence the right people when sculpting a more agile service from the mass of processes that preceded it. And sometimes the right people are surprising people in surprising places.

And so I find myself commending this framework to you along with the narrative that gives it life. I hope you enjoy the ideas and find enough in here to put into practice for yourself. But above all, I hope it encourages you to take a thoughtful approach to the management problems you face, and that you, too, can succeed in teasing them apart. Enjoy ...

# Introduction

Like many books, this one owes a great deal to chance. As a Chief Executive with experience in running viable organisations but in search of a new job, after a year away at Harvard, I found a CEO post in a deeply failing one. Successfully turning that round led to another major assignment to do the same. The second time round I could see there were recurring patterns and some of the management skills required were generic. After that, when I took on a trouble-shooting role helping a very varied mix of struggling organisations analyse and find remedies to their biggest difficulties, the patterns started to present themselves repeatedly and inescapably. I am now into my sixth CEO job (in twenty years) and I've managed every type of organisation: stable, failed, failing, recovering, middle of the road, thriving, and, currently, world-famous and world-leading.

What has struck me again and again is that failure is caused by definable weaknesses in management capabilities, insight and behaviour. Sustained recovery from failure is caused by management with specific positive capabilities, insight and behaviour. And, as I have tried to understand failure, I have discovered how little is written on the subject. There are thousands of management books about success but hardly any about failure, almost as if talking about it risks being infected by it. This is odd given that failure happens so frequently, and to all of us at some point in our lives. Although few of us are unlucky enough to experience out-and-out failure, no one succeeds in business without having made mistakes, and underperformance is a common management concern. So understanding all this is important. My own experience and the wider scrutiny I have carried out have convinced me that by learning from our own and other people's mistakes and failures, and in particular by understanding and adopting the positive capabilities I have been able to identify, you can manage effectively and achieve sustained, long-term success.

So my book, and, in it, the situations I describe and the approaches I advocate, are relevant to everyone who manages: CEOs, consultants, corporate managers responsible for the performance of a team, department, business unit or strategy, as well as entrepreneurs managing their own companies. Some of the examples I use are from large businesses and organisations, but the lessons to be learned from them hold true in much smaller ones, too. On hearing me present my ideas, a consultant working with a firm in the food production industry told me that they were in denial about what was happening to them, and their behaviours exactly mirrored those that I had been describing from my own experience. More than that, the principles are the same for both the private and public sectors and they cross cultures and nations.

# My approach

There is generally a logical, chosen flow to the events that managers encounter. It is their responsibility, using their experience, skills and competence, to manage the sequence of events constructively towards the desired outcome. I show that they can do this, even in what at first sight are very unpromising circumstances. Contrariwise, if they don't shape the sequence of events, it will shape them. That's why terms such as pathway, route, road, process, but also story and narrative recur as explanatory metaphors in what I write. Persisting with just one of those metaphors for a moment, I also point out some absolutely fundamental forks in the road. Recognising they have been reached and acting on them can determine the future pathway the business or organisation follows, with dramatically different, indeed opposite outcomes available.

So my book is about what happens, what to avoid, what to do, how to recognise where a business or organisation is, what help to offer and what to take in the different circumstances that I outline. The pathway to failure and recovery, as well as to avoiding failure, is clear and can be mapped. But it is central to this book that following the pathway, the down and the up, is a matter of choice. Managers and organisations can and must understand the right choices and make them.

This *is not* a book about personal failure and regeneration, or a story of a sinner who repents. It *is* a book about management. The link, though, is simple. Work is a substantial, permanent part of all our lives. What we do in our work and its effects are not different from what we do outside as people. So our work experience is a microcosm of our whole life experience, and organisational failure parallels broader failure, just as individual managerial failure parallels personal failure.

Nor is it an analysis of systems. It is about the fact that management is a highly imperfect science and that businesses – that organisations – go most wrong when managers forget or refuse to acknowledge that. Witness the managerial ethos before the 2008 credit crunch with its breezy arrogance and certainty of superior insight.

This book is a fundamentally practical book in which I draw on:

- my own first-hand experience of turnaround centring on failing hospitals and health care;

- real examples from many arenas – banking, transport, the media, electronics and IT, sport, education, politics, defence – and many countries – the USA, China, Germany, Singapore, Switzerland and more;

- thinkers whose ideas have helped shape my approach, notably Dan Jones, whose 'lean thinking' has had a deep influence on my management techniques, and Steven Pinker, whose insights on organism vs mechanism and nature vs nurture have assisted me in thinking about how organisations work.

# My message

In this book I show that 'failure' is not such a frightening term after all. By taking a long hard look at what is at the heart of failure, analysing its causes and the behaviours of those who cause it, this book will help both established and aspiring managers to cope when things go wrong – as they inevitably do from time to time – and to get out of trouble. A key message is that the sort of failure that we are all likely to face in our working lives is not a catastrophe: the situation can almost always be rescued.

Even more importantly, I show how to avoid those problems in the first place. By reading this book, managers will not only be able to see what else goes wrong when mistakes are made but know how to get it right – with the help of my principles for successful management.

Too often, people make the wrong distinction between failure and success. They see them as simple oppositions but don't actually use them in opposed ways. Most commonly people talk about someone or something being a failure (i.e. a state), whereas something or someone has a success (i.e. reaches an end point). You can and will stick with a failure if you don't do something about it, whereas a success is impressive and laudable but (in its most commonly used meaning) passes quickly. For example, you get sufficiently good A Levels to get you into university but then you have to study at university to get your degree, following which you seek a job to take these skills forward, and so on. If you fail your A Levels and don't do anything else about it, you stay below that threshold, and as judged against that threshold you remain a failure.

Building on this basic distinction, I go on to demonstrate and flesh out my most fundamental point, that there is an opposite state to failure and that simply to define it on the basis of a successful end point misses the point. In contrast, I explore what sustained achievement and being enduringly successful mean, and how you get to them. This is about how to do things, how to behave, how to get on in the long term, so it is overwhelmingly important.

# The book's four parts

- There is a consistent pattern to failure, with different degrees of failure, from a business – or a manager – floundering because they have taken their eyes off the ball, to headline-hitting examples of collapse, all of which provide useful lessons for any manager, whether their organisation is in trouble or not. In **Part 1** of my book I describe what deep failure looks like and how to recognise it, in the form of a simple but original graph which I call the Yosemite curve, with two key variants, total failure (the Niagara drop) and shallow failure (the Panama Canal passage). I go through the six distinct phases to and through failure (struggling, denial, freefall, rock bottom, recovery and consolidation), and the critical points of managerial choice, effort or collusion.

- The good news is that, once you have identified what failure is and what causes it, it becomes possible to find out what can be done to put it right. You can learn from it. You can learn not only how to get out of it but also how to avoid it, as I show in **Part 2** of my book. I describe there the warning signs that indicate that you are running into trouble: how to recognise them, how to tackle their causes and how to avoid further problems. I separate these into passive signs, where lack of insight and action cause the slide into failure, and active signs, where the wrong actions and behaviours actually precipitate failure.

● In **Part 3**, I go through the experience of failure, what it entails, the difficulties you will face, how to cope with the pressures, the crucial communication challenges, and how to start to repair, rebuild, recover and finally consolidate. Organisational chaos is actually the product of complex, purposeful, informed behaviours trying to negotiate blockages caused by others. They don't work because each behaviour is unconnected to the next and typically they frustrate each other, causing ever more complexity and new blockages. Once the behaviours are understood and coordinated they can be redirected and made to work in concert to reduce and then eliminate the chaos. That is the job of a good manager. The people working at Marks & Spencer when it became a failing business a few years ago were broadly the same ones who were there when it became a success again under its new CEO, Stuart Rose. Throughout this period they remained capable and well motivated, but the difference was that it was only with the right guidance and redirection that their efforts achieved the right overall result.

You have to get people to believe that there is a driving force in their business or organisation, which they will then respond to and in so doing take part in creating. In a failed organisation the everyday processes which are vital to its smooth running – for example, people getting together to share problems that run across other areas and to take a shared interest and responsibility in solving them with their shared but different expertise – have ceased to work or are only working mechanistically. This means that no one is controlling them and so those processes are not functioning properly. But the staff have not yet realised that they are not now working properly or how they are not. This has to be put right to move from failure to success, but, if not, that will be what happens.

- In **Part 4** of the book, I give a full and rounded picture of the distinctive skills and behaviours you need as a manager in order to make your organisation thrive. These are specifically not the pursuit of excellence and the outstanding *per se*, which often involve misleading and atypical cases.

For me the crucial insight is that you will inevitably get things wrong and be less than consistently excellent or perfect. But that's OK, as long as you strive relentlessly, accept imperfection, thrive and sustain; as long as you never give up but see one problem solved as the springboard to solving the next. I've made a profit; how do I embed it, how do I increase it, how do I increase market share? I've reduced waits for treatment; how do I eliminate them, how do I give patients choice and discretion for their operation? Try things to see if they succeed and try new things until they do succeed – endless iterations until you get into a virtuous loop. You eat the elephant by dividing it into small pieces and chewing it a bit at a time.

Imperfect managers are the ones who get things done and get things right enough in the real world. I think Jim Collins takes us on the wrong track when he says: 'You can mandate good. Greatness has to be unleashed.' On the contrary, the right measure is not to be an Olympic champion – in each area of endeavour only one person can be that at one time and probably only once. Rather, it is to be a thriving and healthy achiever, as an individual or as a business. And it is much better to release, catalyse and enable 'good' than attempt to mandate it.

# The three critical elements to thrive

That view leads to and forms the central positive of my book: thriving management. Organisations are complex, living entities from which the best results are obtained by tapping into what they and the people in them already know, their underlying experience, skills and wisdom in doing their individual jobs. In order to succeed, managers need to blend and bend these to create a coherent result. But people's behaviours, actions and understandings are not simply explicit and rule driven. They are at least as importantly implicit, instinctive and responsive.

My managerial approach consists of three distinct elements. The first is honesty – with yourself and with others – glaringly simple maybe, but there is lots more to it, as I will show.

The second is total alertness to what is going on, gauging the environment, weighing up what can be done without help and asking for help when it is needed. We've had a run of complaints here. Why? What is the common theme? What are we doing wrong? What has changed? It's about continually choosing where to focus attention and just as importantly where not to, when to reflect and when to act. And an absolutely key part of all this is mastering detail. Too often leadership and top management focus on the big picture, the long term, the strategic at the expense of the immediate and the specific. This is a big mistake. Detail and the big picture are not opposed. They must be aligned. Scan the horizon *and* look at the ground beneath you. When you have done both, you will know how to behave, you will know what you need to do and you will be ready to do it.

The third is coming to terms with and managing what you don't understand and what you can't control. This is the real world, the world of imperfect data, partial understandings and chance discoveries. If you can identify, then describe, then understand an area of the unknown, you make it a known which you then can deal with. So this aspect of management is about continually increasing the area of the known, finding strategies to act on that and looking for further ways to eat away at what appears to be chance, randomness and uncertainty.

# To sum up ...

This is a book for *every* manager. It describes fully and coherently what you need to do and how you need to behave to be a *good* manager and to manage *successfully*. Its route isn't towards perfection or the unattainable. It is about real, hard, sustained achievement. That's what realistic managers need. That's what real managers should go and get.

The book arrives at these key ideas by first looking at managerial, business and organisational failure and their causes. At the book's heart is the belief and the evidence that identifying failure and understanding its root causes is of crucial importance, not just for the obvious reason that it will help to avoid and (if it has happened) get out of failure – which it will – but also because it enables you to establish what the opposite of failure is – what, in short, good management is and how you do it. That is quite a find!

# part one

# Understanding failure

*If we should fail? We fail! But screw your courage to the sticking-place. And we'll not fail.*

WILLIAM SHAKESPEARE, MACBETH

In this first part of the book, I explore what happens to organisations, businesses and institutions during the course of their short or long lives: stability, challenge, disruption, growth, failure, success, maturity, decline, death. Organisations, like people, are mortal and, like people, they live a varied life, with ups and downs, high points and low points. If, as individuals, we obsess about high points, we are seen as drunk or addicted and in denial about the low points that correspond to them. We need the same approach to work, to business, to organisational life. Look at the high points, yes, though without being seduced by them. But even more important, understand the low points so as to avoid them or recover from them. And see where both do and most profitably can fit into a long and healthy business or organisational life.

Failure is where the glaring deficit in understanding is. So I start with that, how it happens, typically suddenly and surprisingly to its victims – but not necessarily to others – and what it looks like and means. Naturally and alongside it, I go through what success means too, but with great caution because I am trying to correct an imbalance in most people's focus on failure and success.

The key to unlocking things is to clarify what the measure or measures of failure and success are, how they are measured, who measures them, and how they change, all of which I explore in the first chapter, with a wide range of vivid examples from every corner of the working world. It may be worth starting with one that blew up in late 2012, relating to the conduct of Jimmy Savile, till his death in 2011, seen as a great entertainer and tireless supporter of good causes, but now exposed as a serial, multiple child abuser and sexual predator. The original measures (entertainer and supporter of good causes) were ones by which he clearly succeeded, but they have been wiped out by one on which he grossly failed (sexual predator). The BBC, probably the most respected broadcasting organisation in the world, came under fire for its allegedly passive toleration of, or unconscious acquiescence in, his behaviour. More than this, in October 2012, its top management reeled under charges that, in late 2011, it had misjudged the seriousness of what had gone on, and had adopted a passive, do nothing approach by not broadcasting a programme which would have opened up investigations into the abuse. This was swiftly followed by a furore over a programme that was actually broadcast in November 2012, making allegations of sexual abuse that were quickly shown to be false. The second on top of the first led to the resignation of the BBC's Director-General of two months, George Entwistle, on 10 November 2012. The measures the BBC were found wanting on were quite different from those used to judge Savile's conduct, but they proved just as potent and their impact was immediate.

In Chapter 2, I set out the recurring pattern and the underlying themes I have found when serious failure – I call it deep failure – occurs. This forms the backbone of the book and the reference point against which I shape my argument. In Chapter 3, I fill out the mainstream case of deep failure by putting it alongside three other possible scenarios: total failure (the end), shallow failure (which we all face and which can be dealt with if we tackle it properly) and, last but not least, a healthy, successful, normal state of affairs. I also describe the possibility – or likelihood – of broad or broadening failure (it may be broad from the outset or may become so), as failure broadens into a general contagion.

1

# Mentioning the unmentionable

We live in a culture that applauds success but is reticent about or glosses over failure; we don't like to talk about it, and in the world of work it is virtually taboo. Try inviting managers and experts to talk about the success of their business, their project or their approach and they will beat a path to your door. Ask them what they got wrong or – when they still had jobs – why they were getting it wrong, and guess the answer you'd get.

Why on reflection isn't that so surprising? Everyone wants to succeed. Everyone wants to feel good about succeeding. It is a bit like the western approach to death. You mustn't mention it, you mustn't discuss it, it is rather impolite. Yet one day it too will affect everyone, and understanding your own mortality is surely a matter of vital importance.

Failure happens. Failure is frequent. Understanding failure is important. 'Failure is success if you learn from it,' says Malcolm Forbes, US billionaire founder of *Forbes* magazine.

People's understandable reluctance to own up to failure may explain why it is so often not properly acknowledged in businesses and in organisations, and why so many managers deny its significance. Judged solely by the relative frequency and the importance of both success and failure in businesses, this is surely odd.

'Failure is not an option', astronaut Gene Kranz's famous phrase, has attained almost mythic status. But Gene was talking about a very specific enterprise, the US Space programme, where a mission failure would be, and in the case of *Challenger* was, catastrophic. Hence the need to mark out a huge gap between failure and success.

More than that, never to acknowledge you have failed may prevent you from recognising how to be truly successful. Jake Burton, owner and founder of Burton Snowboards, said that if his business hadn't almost failed, it wouldn't be the billion-dollar company it became, 'My success is the result of a long series of mistakes.' There's more. According to Reid Hoffman, the very successful founder of LinkedIn, failure needs to be dealt with head on and quickly, 'There's a mantra in the Valley which is "fail fast". ... Tackle the most hard problem that's confronting your business because you will need to know whether you can get through it.' But why stop there? Even if you haven't failed you can still learn from others' mistakes, and from your own. According to Jeff Joerres, CEO of ManpowerGroup, 'If you're not making a mistake a week, you're not learning.'

## What failure looks like

I was asked to look at an organisation which was acknowledged to have gone into deep failure but was now recovering. I interviewed many people who had experienced the organisation in the run-up to and during that failure and here are some of their random comments:

*Bashing my head against a brick wall – chat was useless – inhibited – did not walk the floor – morale was low – 'I say, you do' approach – manager 'a bit of a dinosaur' – closed shop, hush hush, never got to hear what was going on – show run by a cabal – working in silos – people decidedly pissed off – ideas suggested were pooh poohed – in a cocoon.*

*Difficulties were hidden – no safeguard in terms of spending money – rabbit pulled out of the hat on finances – breaking even, then suddenly overspent – brokerage no longer possible, suddenly exposed – bought equipment and facilities we could not afford – met the targets regardless of cost – developed services beyond our capacity – very risky plan – no challenge of the assumptions – the figures were misleading.*

*Got out while the going was good – chose to give the Board only certain information – no challenge – Board were rabbits in the headlights – FD scapegoat – CEO resigned – Chairman asked to leave – lack of control main reason for the problems – we hit rock bottom.*

If you understand failure, you can understand how things go wrong, and why things don't work. If you understand this, you can start to work out ways of avoiding failure. By understanding failure, you can understand how to move on to achieve genuine, deeply rooted, enduring success.

And the word 'success' is also rather ambiguous. It usually means an end point, winning the race and coming first. Less often – but from the point of view of this book, much more interestingly – it includes the process of achieving the win: the effort and the preparation. Even more rarely, and even more interestingly here, it also includes a sense of being *successful*, of sustained achievement. The core of this book is an attempt to locate and describe what creates this *successfulness*, and because success is such an ambiguous term, others are used which are more precise and clear.

You need to look at success and failure together. Separating them leads us to make another big mistake. People often assume that what they learn from success and how they manage success are different from what they learn from failure and how they manage failure. Because the two are reverse sides of the same coin, the opposite is true. Dealing with failure, anticipating it and getting out of it require exceptional management skills – but not unusual ones.

There are two related but also erroneous perceptions:

- firstly, that a failing organisation is different, as if it had leprosy, when in fact the right analogy is with a commonplace curable illness; and

- secondly, that the skills needed to turn things around are different from those needed to keep an organisation on the right track and continuously getting better. Absolutely wrong. They're the same but more strongly etched and more dramatic.

So when does failure occur? It occurs when those in charge fail to ensure that perception and reality are working together in formulating and pursuing business goals, fail to observe the warning signs that things are not as they seem or should be, fail to monitor and review how things are really going against the crucial measures, and so fail to take early corrective action. An example from a very unexpected quarter, legendarily efficient and prudent Switzerland, is a good place to show all this.

# The lesson of Leukerbad

The high Rhône Valley lies at the heart of the Swiss Alps, surrounded by some of the greatest and most beautiful alpine peaks. As you ascend the valley, you pass a small sleepy Swiss town called Leuk. Above Leuk is the spa of Leukerbad, well endowed with natural beauty, mountains and the largest natural spa waters in the Alps, pumping three million litres a day through its various outputs. The spa was the source of the village's historic renown from Roman times and, at the turn of the last century, was a place where the affluent and leisured from across Europe took the waters. But the late twentieth century was different – spas became less fashionable and skiing had taken over. So it was hardly surprising that the great modern tourist trade, which is seen in such famous nearby resorts as Zermatt, Verbier and Gstaad, had largely bypassed Leukerbad.

In the late 1980s Leukerbad elected a new mayor, who felt the time had come for a change. He wanted to develop Leukerbad as a mountain resort and capitalise on its traditional but now slightly worn image. Leukerbad had fantastic natural assets, fantastic potential. Why not use them? So he set about realising that vision. Over the next few years Leukerbad blossomed. It added new ski lifts and developed a good skiing area, and it created beautiful new spa facilities in the hope of recreating – anew – its heyday.

Sadly, though, this story came to light for another reason. That was during the trial of the same mayor of Leukerbad for bankrupting the town and causing the Swiss canton of Wallis (or Valais) to be asked to bail out its multimillion losses. The truth was that the town could not afford its massive investment and it was never likely to provide a reasonable return on it. A compelling vision had blinded its originator – but also others – to harsh reality.

Swiss cantons are truly self-governing and epitomise devolved responsibility. If one place goes bankrupt then all the other communities in the canton must bail it out. And so the rich resorts of Wallis were asked to dig deep to help. Saas-Fee, another ski resort, even contemplated selling its principal asset – its lift company. Eventually, the Swiss courts decided that the banks which had lent the money to Leukerbad were responsible. They therefore suffered instead, but so might have all those other Swiss resorts.

(Epilogue: Leukerbad thankfully recovered from its deep failure and is today a thriving year-round spa resort with hiking in summer and some skiing in winter.)

What went on in Leukerbad is a classic example of failure. But it's not just Leukerbad. It happens everywhere, as I will show throughout this chapter with examples from sport, politics, industry, banking, healthcare, the media and more.

# The omnipresence of failure

Failure isn't rare, it isn't that unusual. It's everywhere, in all corners of the working world. Four varied examples will be enough to show this.

- At the end of the 1990s, Leeds United, one of England's most famous football clubs, was challenging Manchester United and Arsenal, reaching the semi-finals of the European Champions League, the world's premier club competition, when those two very famous clubs didn't. It seemed to be on an unstoppable upward curve. However, it faltered and because the success had been built by overstretching the base resource too far, things went wrong quickly and in a multiple way. Financial problems surfaced and the best players had to be sold. This affected performance, deepening financial problems. More excellent players were sold, making performance even worse, and the depth of the financial problems was revealed as having deteriorated further. Down and down they went, and in May 2007 Leeds were relegated from the second level of English football, and declared themselves bankrupt during the last game of the season. At that time, they were still paying part of the wages of one or more top players whom they had been forced to sell to other clubs years earlier at knock-down prices and on onerous terms. When they filed for bankruptcy in June 2007 with debts of £35 million, they offered to pay their creditors 1p for every pound owed.

- The European consortium-manufactured A380 Airbus was a highly ambitious, high-profile and prestige project, aiming to create the world's biggest passenger airliner, and to push American firm Boeing from its position as the world's leading aeroplane manufacturer by outpacing Boeing's Dreamliner. It went dramatically wrong. The A380 was delivered very late and over budget, precipitating enormous losses and reputational damage. The company had tried to do too much, too soon, and underestimated the complexity of its task and the costs. The A380 problem highlights the fact that major projects have a life, autonomy, complexity and duration that make them resemble actual permanent organisations. Sadly, but importantly, they also resemble organisations in their capacity to go wrong and hurtle into full-blown failure.

- The abject failure of G4S to provide adequate security for the London Olympics, and even worse its failure to realise or acknowledge this till just before the Games began, has had a devastating effect on its reputation, costing it many millions and many future contracts, and leading to the resignation of key senior staff.

- In October 2012 it came to light that the billion-pound tender for the running of the UK's West Coast railway line had been bungled, with an as yet unknown final cost to the taxpayer, but already thought to be in excess of £40 million. Mistakes were made, not realised and/or not acknowledged. The actual quality and the assessed quality of each of the tenders were not the same, as they should have been.

For *all* the organisations people work in, failure is indeed possible. Sometimes it is even probable – according to some estimates, the failure rate for new products is as high as 90%. In certain instances, failure may be inevitable. It can come in many shapes and sizes, but always with very serious consequences.

# Measuring success and failure

Managerial success and failure are typically seen as right and wrong opposites. This is quite misleading and draws us away from key insights we need to manage well. Success is an end point, but management doesn't have an end point. It needs to do what it does well and keep on doing what it does well, achieving particular end points and milestones but not seeing them as the be-all and end-all. It is a common mistake to see particular targets as 'it'. They are not. They are milestones on the road.

It's as if all our doctors and all our medical knowledge were lined up to ensure that we all became super-specimens and won an Olympic gold medal. Not only would that be impossible, because there are not enough Olympic medals to go round, but it would also not be an enduring achievement. Once one stands down from the podium, the effort and experience are over, whereas real life goes on.

When people define success as a clearly understood end point and then go on to describe the qualities of excellence or perfection which will ensure that it is achieved, they are making a fundamental error. Success cannot be pinned down to one thing. Excellence in one context may be mediocrity in another and downright under-performance in a third. Perfection in achieving one goal may mean completely missing the target on another one or even on a variant of the original goal.

People measure success differently depending on what is currently most important to them (and who they are) and also differently at different times. So five key questions to ask are:

1 **Who (i.e. which people and/or groups) are measuring the success?** Is it the user, the customer directly, or is it someone who speaks for them or interprets for them, such as a doctor? Is it the overall paymaster, the regulator, the public, the media?

2 **How are they measuring it?** Direct experience? Second-hand reports? Predictable inspections? Mystery shoppers? Using statistics or complaints?

3 **What are their expectations?** Do they focus on the outcome? (Does it work? Does it make me feel better?) Is cost most

important, assuming the outcome is fine? Do they consider quantity over quality? Variety? Speed, access, waiting and queuing?

4 **What weight should you put on their measurements individually and/or altogether?** Do you share their views yourself? If not, you must be really careful. You must then decide what to do about them, whether and if so how to try to do better in their eyes, and at what cost. This leads to the fifth question which is closely related to this one but not the same. Ask and answer the two questions separately.

5 **How important are their judgements?** Are they something to note or are they crucial? Will they knock you over if you ignore them? Can they alter the context in which you do business?

John Maynard Keynes once said that if you want to pick the winner of a contest, you shouldn't try to pick the person who *you* think is the best (cook, singer, etc.). You should try and pick the one you believe the judges will think the best. In other words, if you want success, you should seek to understand what will maximise your chances of it.

In line with Keynes' comment but contrary to popular misconception, business failure doesn't necessarily entail the failure of *everything*, or even of those elements that in the broadest context might be seen as the most important. To put it more positively, management is about mixing and matching, reviewing and often compromising. This means it's about continuously recalibrating: I thought this was the 100 metres. I now realise it's the shot putt. Here are six very varied examples which show that the measure of success isn't necessarily obvious or straightforward, that it needs proper analysis, and that it varies:

- A few years ago when Marks & Spencer ran into serious trouble it was still selling premium-quality clothing and food. But it was not doing what its customers, its investors or the stock market expected of it, which was to be clearly ahead of its rivals as a marque of choice: superior in quality and totally reliable. Customers therefore began to vote with their feet and drift towards competitors, and the company's profits fell. Under the leadership of Stuart Rose it turned itself around and became thriving and healthy because he tackled the source of the problem and met the crucial expectations of its stakeholders.

- Success for the Pakistan cricket team is different from success for the Irish cricket team. Cricket is *the* sport in Pakistan; in Ireland it hardly figures. If Pakistan beats Ireland at cricket, it is no big deal, but if it loses, as it did in the 2007 World Cup in Jamaica, this is a disaster and represents a complete failure. Conversely, if Ireland had lost to Pakistan in Jamaica then it would not have been a failure or a disaster because it would have been expected and predictable. When Ireland won, it was a great triumph because the team was exceeding reasonable expectations. If the Irish cricket team was judged on whether it could beat Pakistan routinely, then we would be consigning it to permanent failure, which is neither necessary nor helpful, nor indeed true. In fact the Irish team was quickly knocked out of the competition. But no matter: in Ireland, it was still a triumph.

- Britain's lone ski jumper in the Calgary Winter Olympics was Eddie Edwards, known worldwide as Eddie the Eagle. He finished last in the Olympic ski jump, by a long way. But he did finish the twelfth best in the world and he had had no support and the most incredible obstacles to overcome. Failure or success?

- The measurement issue emerges very clearly in politics. Was Bill Clinton almost impeached because his policies and actions to safeguard America abroad and to improve it at home were wrong? No, this was a measurement based on rules of conduct, which no one would have expected to prove critical when he was elected.

- Kerala is a southern Indian state with a 30 million population. In India many people have to beg and live on virtually nothing. A substantial minority of the population, higher among women, still cannot read: and basic healthcare is not available to many. Although Kerala is in resource terms fairly typical, there is virtually no begging, there is universal literacy and a healthcare system that reaches and covers everyone. It does not have the lavishness or all the facilities of a full-blown western system, but it certainly looks like success on any reasonable metric of what Kerala could be asked to achieve.

- The USA spends 16–17% of its gargantuan GDP on healthcare, but 20% of the population does not have basic healthcare insurance, so they cannot get all the treatment they need, unless they are able to find money they don't have. There are no waiting lists, or at least there are apparently none. The USA has state-provided health insurance coverage for the over 65s – Medicare – but if you are 60 or 61 with inadequate or no insurance and a hip problem, what can you do? Create your own waiting list and wait 4 or 5 years until you are entitled to Medicare. Cancer treatment is very good – if you can afford it. Paying for it bankrupts nearly 20% of cancer patients and their families. Is that success?

## Measuring the successfulness of the Olympic Games

The Olympic Games provide useful insights into success and failure, not as a sport but as a sequence of enormously large projects:

- The Chinese did not let themselves be driven by cost for the 2008 Beijing Olympics, and they were a great success: spectacular, well organised and a showcase for China. Certainly they could have been put on more cheaply, with much tighter budgets, but would they have been so successful?
- Equally, bankrupting a city or saddling it with debts for the next 30 years – as happened with the Montreal Olympics in 1976 – can only be deemed a failure.
- In the debates over the staging of the Olympics, there always seems to be a strain of opinion that wants to ignore cost. This is the strain that left Athens with a range of beautiful but unusable facilities after the 2004 games.
- This strain also dismisses concern over the 400% inflation in the cost of the Olympic swimming pool for 2012, saying in defence that 'London needs a Zaha Hadid' (the world-famous Iraqi architect who designed the Olympic swimming pool)' and 'good work doesn't come cheap'. Indeed it does not, but the Olympics are not principally about great architecture and the work does have to be paid for.

In the case of hosting the Olympics, then, success should be measured as a long-term positive legacy for the host city and an improved image worldwide. If that is the right measure, the initial verdict on the London games must be positive. They achieved their key objectives: construction and spending on time and within budget; a huge public appetite for tickets; a permanent legacy in the rejuvenation of a depressed part of east London; the best, most watched Paralympics ever; a positive sense of London and the UK conveyed worldwide; and a lifting of national pride and the national spirit.

What I have tried to show in this section is that if your business or your organisation is to succeed, you and it cannot have a rigid, fixed idea of success in advance. Success in a particular role, task or endeavour depends on the current circumstances, varies with time and typically depends on the changing views of others. That doesn't mean you shouldn't start with the best idea you can of what your goal of success looks like – you should. It does mean you should test it and recalibrate it using the aids I have set out and bearing in mind the sort of examples I have given. That way you will set out on the right road.

# Misrepresenting success and failure

Now look at another aspect. Not telling the truth about what you are doing and your real achievements will almost inevitably ultimately lead to failure. I will show how and why in the next chapter. Here are four graphic and varied examples:

- In recent years, there have been many allegations and some convictions relating to cheating and match fixing in sport. It wasn't a success when Ben Johnson won the 100 m at the Seoul Olympics only to be discovered to have been taking drugs, because what we thought was happening and what was actually happening were different. In cricket, some offences led to criminal charges, conviction and jail. Lance Armstrong's unprecedented string of victories in the Tour de France weren't successes as they were drug supported, in a sport where it now appears that drug taking was rife. In such cases, the failure extends well beyond the individual and casts a shadow over the whole sport. This sort of failure is very infectious.

- The UK government had to make an announcement about transport which reflected badly on it and its policies. The idea was to get it out without anyone noticing it was that bad. One advisor, Jo Moore, suggested that one day would be a good day on which to bury bad news. The email in which she suggested this became public knowledge within a couple of days and created an absolute furore. The reason was that the day in question was 11 September 2001, the day on which two passenger jets were flown into New York's Twin Towers causing their demolition and the deaths of nearly 3,000 people. Within a fairly short time, the reaction to the memo led to Ms Moore's resignation, followed a little later by that of the Secretary of State. The chief press officer left the department, as did the Permanent Secretary, Sir Richard Mottram, the top senior official there. His comment on hearing what had happened was: 'We're all ****ed, I'm ****ed, you're ****ed, the whole department's ****ed. It's been the biggest cock-up ever and we're all completely ****ed.'

- The phone hacking scandal in the UK has led to the demise of the *News of the World* newspaper, severely damaged the reputation of the titan News International Corporation and many key figures currently or previously within it, has led to a string of prosecutions and has extended to other papers and media corporations. Its impact will probably change the face of media reporting in the light of the Leveson Inquiry recommendations. Once again we can see that an offence is bad, but concealment is much worse, if, as is likely, maybe inevitably, the concealment is unmasked.

- During the writing of this book, more examples of the failure I'm identifying came to light and continue to come to light in the worlds of banking and finance than in any other. Many focused on the convulsions of the credit crunch of late 2008, but many did not: Barings Bank, Bear Stearns, Royal Bank of Scotland, Société Générale, UBS, Barclays. Some are about being caught out by events, but others are about breaking rules, deception and dishonesty: examples include LIBOR manipulation by banks, and banks illegally harbouring drug and other money, and failing to give a true and fair account of clients' finances.

What I am saying in this section is that, at the end of the day, success and failure are real things based on real achievements or the lack of them. In the previous section I showed that you must understand what they are. In this one I have tried to show that understanding them isn't enough. You must respect, accept and follow them. If you don't, if you try to give the impression that you are doing what you should, but actually aren't, then sooner or later you will come a cropper – and a big one. So don't go down this road. It is the road to ruin.

# The infectiousness of failure

Both from personal experience, coming into 'failing' organisations which I have then had to manage, and also going round others in trouble or hearing from those who work in them, a frequent refrain is: 'It's nothing to do with us. We're doing a perfectly good job, as dedicated, competent professionals. This is just about management games and silly rules.'

These people are wrong. It's a defence mechanism, it's a delusion, and it's an illusion. If an organisation is failing on the measures that are at that point in time regarded as key by those who are in a position to judge, then it is indeed failing. If nothing is done about that then, irrespective of all those other good things going on which may be at the very core of the organisation's purpose, its failure will deepen.

Just as some Manchester United players might still be great players when the club is seen to be failing, so it can be with, for example, hospital doctors. When I became CEO of the Royal United Hospital in Bath, we were undoubtedly the poorest-performing hospital in England, with patients waiting much longer for treatment than anywhere else. Doctors pointed out to me that the hospital had the lowest patient death rate of any general hospital in the country and that you were 20% less likely to die there than in an average general hospital, let alone a less safe one. This was an absolutely tremendous testament to the staff and one of the pillars upon which we built the recovery of the hospital, but it did not alter the fact that it was failing.

The staff – even key staff – who make the comment that it's nothing to do with them, are not facing up to reality. What is true is that it isn't their fault. But they do get demoralised, they retreat into their corners, they are well aware of the measures that are being used. Partly because they separate themselves from the other world of the organisation and hide in their corners and partly because this other world of the organisation is not functioning or is collapsing, many of the things that underpin their practice, their work and their outcomes begin to degrade. Inevitably and inexorably, people's work, people's commitment and people's output also start to decline and degrade.

So, in this section I have tried to show that, although the causes and the measures of failure are typically restricted and specific, its effects are not. They spread and spread, corroding the morale, the workings and the effectiveness of an organisation, until something is done to begin to put it right, to start on the road to recovery.

# To sum up …

Failure is out there waiting for everyone. It is an everyday fact and an everyday reality. In order to be successful, you must avoid being surprised by it and caught out by it. If you are prepared for the possibility and, sooner or later, the likelihood of failure coming, and work out exactly what the measures of success and failure are, you will be able to take steps to avoid it.

So, ensure you have got a grip on how success is judged, which means how it is measured:

- Don't assume you know what the critical measures of success are for you, in this situation, here and now. Test your starting assumptions in the way I have described in the chapter. That way you will get to the actual measures of success.

- Look hard and see who has the right, the legitimacy, the need, the power, the influence or the will to create the measures, what they are saying, what they are doing and what their behaviour is. This will reveal what the measures are.

- Don't just rely on your own judgement. Find out what others whose insight you respect (and who are sympathetic to your desire to work this out) think are the measures of success and compare them with yours. With a little constructive toing and froing, you should quickly get a high degree of consensus between their and your views. Then you can be fairly sure you're right.

- Be alert to the fact that you've identified what the measures are, here and now. Tomorrow and somewhere else they will be subtly, perhaps radically, different. Keep your antennae up all the time, watching out for this potential change.

My aim is to help you to know clearly what the measures of success are and who is judging them. If you do, then not only have you got the best chance of satisfying them, you may be able to start a positive dialogue to alter the measures and the judgements so that they make better sense – and work more to your and your business's benefit.

In the next chapter I will bring all this much closer to home.

# 2

# The pattern of failure: the Yosemite curve

Field Marshal Montgomery famously said that 'the great thing about doing no preparation is that failure comes as a complete surprise', and failure does indeed come as a great surprise. But why should that be, why does it catch us unawares and make us realise that the situation we are in is different, quite different, from what we'd thought? The element of surprise is important because there isn't typically a slow, gradual slide into failure. Again and again managers, people, businesses, organisations think they're all right, then all of a sudden, too late, they realise they are a long, long way from that. They are not progressing gently downhill but cascading unstoppably.

When I first became CEO of an organisation that everyone agreed was failing, I noticed some unusual features: widespread misjudgement of the problems faced, a failure to respond to what the external world, customers and stakeholders were saying, blindness to the consequences of major actions and no one ensuring that staff had the right skills, were directed in the right way, and were monitored to see that they actually achieved. Dealing with my second failing organisation, I realised there were recurring features: firstly the discontinuity between performing satisfactorily and failing to do so, and then the realisation that there was a common path that organisations went through when they went into deep failure and lost control of their own destiny.

I've seen at close quarters more than 20 organisations experiencing failure. I've been able to refocus on key aspects of failure, confirm the repeating pattern and understand what is common to all of them. I have also checked this out with colleagues who have experienced failure directly by being in the middle of failing organisations, or indirectly as outside observers and rescuers.

My conclusion is that there is a characteristic path of organisational or business failure with characteristic features and pitfalls, and a right way to get out at the other end. I've mapped this on a curve which I call the Yosemite curve. I call it that quite simply because it reminds me of the asymmetrical profile of that stunningly beautiful Californian valley with the steep face of El Capitan to the left.

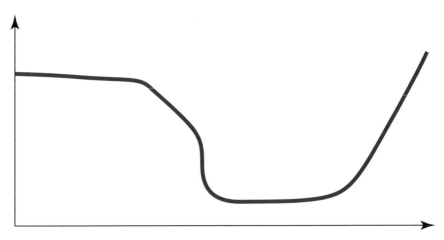

*The Yosemite curve*

I divide the failure process into six different phases. To analyse these phases I map the performance of an organisation over time against acceptable, required performance. The key to unlocking the failure pattern is not just to draw a graph of performance but to compare it with something else that is closely related to performance and ideally should be identical to it, but isn't necessarily. Quite simply it is what the performance is thought to be, i.e. the perception of performance. I decided to map 'actual performance' and 'perceived performance' together because what I kept seeing was a marked divergence between them as failure hit an organisation, as it went through failure and as it tried to come out of failure. It struck me that there was a key message in this. The graph is on the next page.

The graph divides neatly and naturally into time periods. The first is the period of acceptable performance. I call this phase zero as it relates to the normal and normally permanent state of affairs. Phase 1 is when there starts to be a divergence, however gentle and gradual, from that state, where an organisation starts to struggle. Phase 2 covers the period when it is already hurtling into failure but this is not universally apparent. Phase 3 traces the period when the failure is public but remedial action isn't taken. Phase 4 describes a period of stability, but a very dismal stability with completely unsatisfactory and unacceptable levels

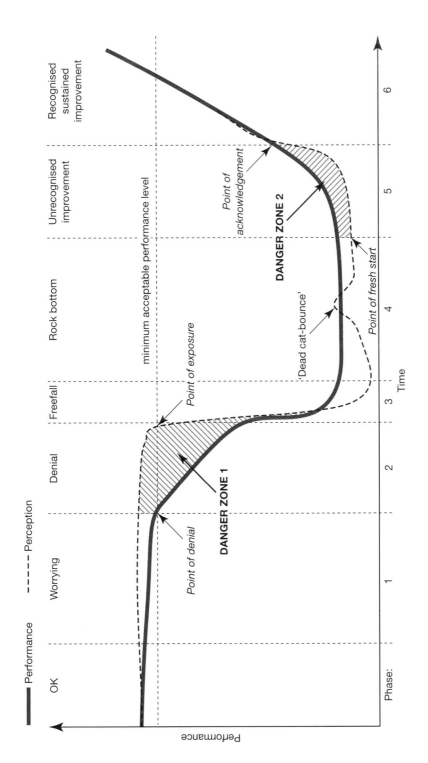

The six phases of the failure process

of performance; the organisation is at rock bottom. Phase 5 describes the first stirrings of recovery and then of steady improvement. Phase 6 describes acknowledged improvement and the regaining of autonomy and embedding of good performance, but this time with an upward momentum partly derived from the experience of what has happened and the insight derived from that. This typically distinguishes this phase from the performance prior to failure.

I set out the six phases in the table below, corresponding to the graph, and highlighting four key points where the failure path 'turns'.

- The first, the **point of denial**, is where performance is no longer acceptable but this is covered up or denied: phase 1 turns into phase 2.

- The second is the **point of exposure** where any cover-up is revealed: phase 2 turns into phase 3 and the organisation hits rock bottom (phase 4).

- The third turning point is when there is a **fresh start** and the organisation begins to recover: phase 4 becomes phase 5.

- The final turning point, the **point of acknowledgement**, is the point at which it becomes generally and widely recognised that the organisation is now healthy and thriving, performing as it should: phase 5 turns into phase 6. How the organisation is being managed through all this is vitally important, so I have characterised the management approach being taken in each phase.

| | SIX PHASES OF A FAILING ORGANISATION | KEY CHANGES, REALITY OR PERCEPTION | THE PHASES |
|---|---|---|---|
| 1. | Organisation with remediable problems | | Reactive |
| | | ◄─── Point of denial | |
| 2. | Denial, concealment, error, lying | | Passive |
| | | ◄─── Point of exposure | |
| 3. | Freefall | | Absent |
| 4. | Rock bottom – hopeless and helpless | | Active but directionless |
| | | ◄─── Point of fresh start | |
| 5. | Unrecognised or undervalued improvement | | Proactive |
| | | ◄Point of acknowledgment | |
| 6. | Acknowledged improvement | | Innovative |

*The six phases of deep failure*

Here are some key guiding assumptions that underpin the graph:

- Every business, every organisation with significant tasks, from time to time faces difficulties and problems that it cannot immediately resolve. These are part and parcel of its daily business and do not mean the organisation is failing. Each year, it is typically quite a challenge to make enough profit (or, in the public sector, balance the books) and meet the key targets that are seen as defining success. Sometimes soundly functioning organisations will miss a particular target.

- But there are businesses and organisations, which are not only not coping with difficulties but have lost the ability to do so.

- An organisation's or a business's performance and the perception of its performance should be identical or at least reasonably close.

- When the two diverge, with performance materially worse than it seems to be, it is a strong indication either that the business or organisation is already failing or that this divergence will actually become a cause of failure. This is my key finding.

- After a business has 'failed' and is starting to recover, the perception of its improving performance typically lags behind the reality. This is dangerous and a brake on improvement.

# Phase 1: Struggle

Organisations manage satisfactorily. Organisations struggle. Organisations have problems. But the first defining point in moving from (normal) struggle to (abnormal) failure is the lack of acknowledgement that significant problems remain, are mounting or even exist. This is the point of denial. This is when an organisation with remediable problems (phase 1) starts to become a failing organisation (phase 2). It moves from struggle to denial, from puzzlement to concealment, from dismay to disinterest. This is disastrous.

People can walk into this. In some organisations I have worked in and with, with a glaring financial problem, while detailed plans have been put together to remedy it (still in phase 1 and aiming to stay there), the plans remained theoretical, they were not realistic, they were designed to impress and mollify others rather than to be realistically implementable and achievable. The result: initial acknowledgement begins to turn into denial and/or delusion, and as these plans fail or fall short, a little time has been gained but that time has not been used as it should have been, to get working on the real, feasible solution. The business has now moved to the brink of phase 2.

At the next iteration the same thing is likely to happen (plausible but unrealistic plans), but this time there will be more cynicism among those asked to implement the plans and even less scope to do so. It is now virtually inevitable that the business will be plummeting into deep failure (phase 2) because the only way out, admitting difficulty, seeking external aid and working on a different approach, is not being tried and is closed off.

# Phase 2: Denial

In phase 2, the organisation is on a very dangerous declining trajectory – perception and reality have now separated. Those within the organisation who could highlight the problem choose not to do so. Those who ought to be becoming aware of it are not. In the meantime the causes are magnifying the problem. This phase can go on for some months but it is a very unstable situation and it is virtually inevitable that it will come to an end for one of the following reasons:

- Those responsible for the problems but who have actually given up on them will flee.

- Someone will blow the whistle on the problem, causing those responsible to be removed from the scene. For example, according to a report in the *Guardian* dated 26 March 2011, 'The managers of Madonna's charity in Malawi have been ousted after they squandered $3.8 m on a school that will never be built. The damning audit came as Raising Malawi confirmed that it has scrapped plans for a $15 m elite academy for girls. In its report it [the Global Philanthropy Group] said the [CEO's] level of mismanagement and lack of oversight was extreme.'

- The problems will become so obvious and large that concealment and denial will no longer be possible, again causing removal of those responsible. There are numerous recent examples of this in the world of city trading: Nick Leeson, Barings Bank, losses $1.4 billion (1995); Yasuo Hamanaka, Sumitomo, losses $2.6 billion (1996); John Rusnak, Allied Irish Banks, losses $691 million (2002); Jérôme Kerviel, Société Générale, losses $6.3 billion (2008); David Higgs, Credit Suisse, losses $2.65 billion (2008); Kweku Adoboli, UBS, losses $1.5 billion (2011); Bruno Iksil in London and his boss, Ina Drew, known as the Queen of Wall Street, JPMorgan, losses of more than $2 billion (2012). (Figures as reported in the press).

There are two variants of the perception and reality split which happens in this phase, the first based on deception, and the second – the more common – based on delusion.

# Phase 3: Freefall

When an organisation gets into this position, it is awful and it feels awful – for everyone. No one knows what to do. No one is trusted. The organisation has lost coherence. Blame is everywhere. The organisation has lost autonomy and is directed what to do.

I was asked to help a well-known organisation facing adverse publicity about a really problematic issue. A few days later, one of my staff was told by a senior manager working there, but accountable to an organisation outside it and overseeing its problems, that they were totally preoccupied in dealing with the immediate problem. At that moment it would be highly inconvenient to have anyone else coming in. I rang the CEO. His response was 'Yes, I am sorry about that. But you need to understand the position we are in. We have people from outside directing this process. We are not in control of it. Where we are now, I need permission to go to the toilet, and I am the CEO!'

What does it feel like in a failing organisation? There will be a siege mentality because there *will* be a siege. A sense of rudderlessness, hopelessness and helplessness will permeate everything. People have stopped believing things can be done. They will have retreated into their corners and be doing what they can there and nowhere else. The organisation will be very confused about its current obligations, but they are very likely to be impossible to meet.

So, there seems to be no coherent way forward: the previous rationale for doing pretty well everything is likely to have collapsed with nothing to replace it. At this point not only is there no direction in the organisation, there is no pretence of it. As underlying problems are not dealt with they get worse at an alarming rate. This is the phase in which everyone in the organisation and everyone outside recognises that something is drastically amiss.

What had seemed just about acceptable is shown suddenly and spectacularly to be completely unacceptable, as the true state of the organisation is revealed – and that it is dramatically different from what was thought.

When this happens – be it in the private sector, as with Northern Rock and Enron, or in the public sector, as with the publication in 1998 of the report into the deaths of several children undergoing heart surgery at the Bristol Royal Infirmary, in which it emerged that warning signal after warning signal had been ignored – a furore follows.

Take the case of Bear Stearns. In March 2008 the US financial giant collapsed. The bank's value plummeted to $250 million compared to $14 billion the previous year (and the share price fell by a factor of 30 in a month), leaving a failed shell of an organisation. But up until the week before the collapse, people at Bear Stearns, including its CEO, were saying that 'everything was fine' and it faced no liquidity issue. Within a very short period of time its CEO resigned, and it was preyed upon and swallowed up.

Revelations about the manipulation of LIBOR rates at Barclays emerged in the summer of 2012, and clearly demonstrated the Yosemite curve's 'point of exposure'. Within a week of them becoming known the CEO, Chair and COO resigned, the revelation caused a firestorm in the media and in Parliament – with the contagion spreading to a slew of banks, indicating a deep failure across the banking system. On 17 July 2012, the Governor of the Bank of England poured further fuel on the flames as he testified before a parliamentary committee about warnings he had given and others' failure to listen to them: more exposure.

That day and the next vividly demonstrated that the point of exposure happens a lot. Across the Atlantic, a Senate subcommittee was grilling HSBC officials about enormous and routine money laundering, notably of drug money. And right in the middle of the hearing, at a true point of exposure, the Head of Compliance at HSBC resigned while giving his evidence, clearly because of what he was revealing.

Still the same day and back across the Atlantic in England, the CEO of G4S was being grilled by another parliamentary subcommittee for his company's failure to provide enough security staff for the London Olympics, with everyone only realising this about two weeks before the Games began. In addition to receiving withering personal attacks from MPs, the CEO and G4S were mercilessly criticised across the board by all the media and, given that the Olympics are a world-wide phenomenon, across the world, with devastating effects on their reputation.

Quite simply, outsiders lose confidence at a stroke and, with it, trust. They feel the organisation is hopeless in all respects. That's why:

- There were queues outside Northern Rock after its finances unravelled, with investors panicking to withdraw their money, irrespective of all assurances that it was safe.

- Patients wanted to go anywhere but Maidstone Hospital after 90 patients had died after contracting the 'superbug' *Clostridium difficile*.

- I was told when taking over my first failing organisation 'At its best this hospital is never more than mediocre in anything it does.' Yet there was much about the hospital that was far from mediocre, as I quickly discovered.

Such reactions conspire to make matters worse, by causing the failed organisation to be blamed for practically everything, including much it may never have been guilty of. By the time their failings had been exposed, the Northern Rock savings were actually secure and the patients at Maidstone were as safe there as anywhere else.

## Blame culture at the Royal United Hospital, Bath

I had a taste of being blamed for everything at the Royal United Hospital, Bath. I'd been there for a matter of days when I was asked to attend a meeting as sole representative of the hospital with our partner organisations and the Health Authority, the senior organisation to which we were all accountable. The meeting itemised a series of problems. At the end of each discussion item, people in the room turned to me and said 'so what are you going to do about it?' I began to realise that there were ten people in the room, only one of whom had no responsibility for the problems Bath was facing: that person was me. It was then I realised that in order to move Bath forward I had to alter the terms of engagement with our partners and others to give us the freedom to move on and not to be blamed for things that we were not responsible for. Although it was hard, I did just that – and it made a huge difference. The hospital, and everyone working in it, could move on.

What causes exposure is usually one of three things: a discrepancy on resources (meaning money); under-achievement on outputs (volumes, targets); or a failure in terms of outcomes, usually involving harm, lack of safety, effectiveness or quality. The money examples are everywhere but famous recent ones include the American financiers Bernie Madoff and Allen Stanford who took investors' money and spent it on themselves rather than investing it, in the hope that new investors would continue to bankroll the deception. Both men are now serving long jail sentences.

In the public sector achieving targets is often viewed as a key imperative. The penalties for failing can be severe and not surprisingly most organisations achieve them. However, there are highly publicised cases of such organisations apparently achieving targets but in fact deluding themselves, manipulating their figures, not telling the whole truth or actually lying about their position in order to appear to meet them.

This syndrome is typically triggered by excessive pressure to achieve without the accompanying wherewithal, leading to a frightened or actually dishonest response (or both) by someone in the accountability chain pretending they have achieved something they haven't. This deception then becomes ingrained and over a period of time others collude and the reality moves further and further from what is being presented. Nick Leeson did it at Barings Bank and many of those fixing LIBOR rates did it too. As the truth has emerged, organisation after organisation has fallen into deep failure. Resignations, public crises, charges of fraud, prosecution, conviction often follow. Morale falls through the floor. And because systems have been misused or set up to create a false picture, processes will not be working properly and delivery will be imperilled.

Objective and reality are turned on their heads so that in this delusional or denying world the objective defines the reality instead of reality defining the objective. We want unreliable and thus high-cost mortgages to be reliable and therefore cheap, so we will put them through an arcane and impenetrable rebranding process and … hey presto! Subprime mortgage lending. We want interest rates to be lower or higher, so in setting LIBOR we will say they are and they will be. Unfortunately the fiction has to come to an end sooner or later, as it did in both cases. And the later, the worse.

Outcome delusion or denial often applies to clinical failures, typically involving patient harm or even death, and can precipitate organisational failure. In the Bristol Royal Infirmary in the mid-1990s heart operations kept being done on children even though the mortality rate was much higher than in other hospitals. The hospital convinced itself that these outcomes – these deaths – were acceptable and defensible, and found explanations and excuses to justify them. It would not listen, and strongly resisted other less favourable explanations. When it finally came to public notice just how bad the outcomes were, how many children had died, and the unacceptability of the practice, it led to one of the most profound organisational changes in the history of the NHS. The effect on Bristol was devastating. It was publicly shamed and on the floor.

# Phase 4: Rock bottom

The organisation hits rock bottom very quickly. There is now no concealment that there is no action. The organisation is totally reactive as it has lost all sense of direction. At this point it has moved to phase 4 – stuck on the bottom with low morale.

This is when it is at maximum risk of blame and has minimum ability to defend itself. There is an over-reaction: those who have missed the tell-tale signs now see tell-tale signs everywhere. The organisation, metaphorically unconscious on the floor, is blamed not just for all its own failures but often for many failures which are not its fault. I remember observing in one organisation that it seemed to be blamed for the fact that it had rained yesterday!

At this time people other than management, the board or outside interested parties, if the failure is spectacular enough, start to push the organisation to deliver immediate outputs. They may even provide short-term fixes, but they are external and alien and as soon as the fix is withdrawn, the problem returns – it was never fixed in the first place.

This is my take on what is known in financial circles as the 'dead cat bounce' and is shown on the Yosemite curve as a little bump in the flat lining that characterises phase 4. (The rather grisly metaphor refers to what would supposedly happen if a cat were dropped from a Wall Street skyscraper: it would indeed bounce but it would nonetheless be dead.) The organisation is effectively moribund but is being pushed by people remote from it to satisfy short-term imperatives that do nothing to improve real performance. Permanent improvement will only be achieved by fundamentally reviewing and redesigning the underlying systems and, critically, embedding the skills needed to manage the good, new systems in the permanent staff.

# Phase 5: Recovery

What can and does improve performance is the introduction of effective new management, bringing with it effective new direction. Improvement takes some time because analysis of and response to immediate problems have to come first. If the new regime isn't up to solving the problems or doesn't go about things in the right way, the business will remain at 'rock bottom' (phase 4) until it gets a regime that can actually tackle things.

All that said, a competent new regime will start to make a difference relatively quickly. In later chapters I will describe this process and the management skills and tactics needed to bring about the improvement. Performance will, at first slowly, but nonetheless steadily, improve.

Phase 5 can also be dangerous. Performance is now actually better than practically everyone, particularly those judging from outside, think it is. This typically acts as a significant drag factor on the improvement because once again much effort has to go into managing perception rather than reality: in other words, the sceptics have to be shown in unequivocal terms that material, positive changes are taking place and are impacting positively on performance. There are very understandable reasons for scepticism, though they are not necessarily good ones. Those charged with monitoring and scrutinising the business's performance may be frightened or wary. They were late in seeing how problematic it was and will naturally believe that it is much more dangerous for them to get caught a second time. The result: they tend to underestimate what is going on and react accordingly.

At the Royal United Hospital, Bath, for example, although we had made major improvements, I was told that if I continued to exaggerate them, the Health Authority would publicly dissociate itself from us. It took quite an effort both to continue to demonstrate the improvement publicly and then to show them that any exaggeration was not ours but the media's. We did, however, manage it, so you can get through this, if you have a good story to tell.

# Phase 6: Consolidation

Phase 5 need not be static, but, sadly, it can go on for a long time. The business's successes are slowly realised but often too little and too late. The best way out of this is a performance epiphany or event, which spectacularly demonstrates to those outside that the world has indeed changed. Once that happens the organisation is back in the normal world: performing reasonably and seen to be performing reasonably – phase 6.

I remember vividly this happening at Medway at a meeting with our senior government monitor. He first, slightly grudgingly, noticed minor improvements in our waiting times, then realised they were very major indeed; then, when we explained how we had achieved them, he realised that we had in fact implemented a pioneering management system. After that he asked us if we would become national exemplars. All this took place in one meeting (a full account of this appears on page 109).

Though Bear Stearns certainly was a failure, JPMorgan picked it up with the aim of putting it back together. The buyer knew what it was doing. It was getting, according to the *Financial Times*, 'a prime brokerage business, a large franchise with a promising future' – and at a bargain-basement price. It judged that the company was remediable and recoverable.

The London Millennium Dome, built by the last UK Labour government, cost about $1 billion but signally failed to meet PM Tony Blair's aim that it should be 'a beacon to the world', and was perceived post-millennium as a classic white elephant. It was eventually sold to Anschutz Entertainment Group at a knock-down price and it has now been successfully redeveloped as a profitable and once more iconic indoor entertainment arena.

## To sum up ...

There is a clear, predictable pattern to failure, how it happens and what its course is, and the key clue in the pattern is that the perception of performance and the reality of performance move dramatically apart. This is unsustainable and precipitates deep or fundamental failure. The Yosemite curve tracing failure divides into six phases, through the fall, to the bottom and into recovery.

Understand this pattern, understand the phases and what moves you from one phase to the next, and you will have a sound basis for understanding how and why failure happens, how to get out of it and how to avoid it in the first place. In the remainder of the book, I set out the skills and behaviours you will need to do just that.

# 3

# Other types of failure

In the preceding pages I have described the pattern of **deep failure**, the classic form of failure which almost everyone can recognise. I did this by drawing on my own experience, generalised and validated by others' experiences and examples from elsewhere. As I have thought and learnt more, I have refined and extended my analysis of failure. I still believe that the account of deep failure I have given is central, but I have now identified two other 'failure' pathways leading in quite different directions, which it is vital to understand. One is more severe than deep failure. It is irrecoverable and I call it **total failure**. The other is less severe and avoids the major, adverse effects of failure. I call it **shallow failure**. The three types of failure sit next to each other. Absolutely crucially, you can shift upwards or slip downwards from one type to another, beneficially from deep to shallow, disastrously from shallow to deep, and terminally from deep to total. Later on I will show how to avoid slipping, how to keep failure shallow and how to avoid it altogether.

I have also identified a very important variant of deep failure, where it becomes clear that the failure is much wider than initially thought, and not just about one business or organisation but a failure on the part of a whole group of businesses or of a sector. Because it will cover a broad swath of organisations, I call it **broadening failure**.

## Total failure: the Niagara drop

The simplest of the two other failure pathways to observe, and one that requires less time to discuss because of its finality, is the pathway to failure from which there is no return, the 'extinction' trajectory. This describes a case where the failure continues so long and is so total that it is irrecoverable. I call it the Niagara drop partly because that is what the graph looks like but also because it is only finally discovered when, metaphorically, the boat goes over Niagara Falls and is smashed to pieces. Someone has to pick up the wreckage but no one seriously tries to put the boat back together again. Mercifully this is very rare.

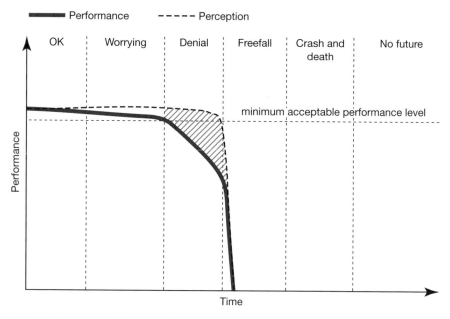

Total failure: the Niagara drop

As recounted in the film *Rogue Trader*, in 1995 at the investment bank Barings Bank, Nick Leeson lost £827 million, mainly on the futures markets, betting against Japan. By the time anyone discovered what he had done, he had betted away all the company's assets. The bank went bust. Some pieces were picked up but it was hardly a 'recovery' in a recognisable sense: failure had gone too far for too long.

The energy firm Enron collapsed in 2001 when it became clear that it had used dubious, illegal and completely misleading accounting practices to underpin its apparent financial position. Enron was bankrupted and disappeared. But perhaps of even more general interest here, its auditors, Arthur Andersen, then one of the world's top five accountancy and audit firms, was caught in the maelstrom. It was charged and found guilty of obstruction of justice for shredding thousands of documents and deleting emails in the company's files that tied the firm to its audit of Enron. Although this ruling was later overturned by the US Supreme Court, by then the firm had lost the majority of its customers and had shut down with 85,000 people losing their jobs.

At the beginning of October 2012, allegations began to proliferate of child sex abuse by the late Sir Jimmy Savile who in his lifetime had become known and loved, initially as a famous presenter and entertainer, but then as a great fund raiser for charity and supporter of good causes. One result of the allegations is that the two major charities set up in his name have decided that, as donations will be severely hit, they should close down.

In the three cases of Enron, Arthur Andersen and the Savile charities, the reason for total failure is the complete loss of reputation. To put it another way, perception and reality had drifted irrevocably apart and could not be put together again.

Here is a completely different example showing what can happen in the public or charitable sector. A project funded by Madonna's charity, Raising Malawi, to create an Academy School for Girls in Malawi was abandoned despite the fact that $3.8 million had been spent. It had not broken ground; there was no title to the land; Trevor Neilson, a founder of the group, was reported in *The New York Times* as saying that there was 'overall a startling lack of accountability on the part of the management in Malawi and the management team in the United States'; the executive director was described as unable to 'effectively manage project plans, people and finances'; the head of the school-to-be's 'charisma masked a lack of substantive knowledge of the practical application of educational development, and her weak management skills were a major contributor to the current financial and programmatic chaos'. Added together all these failings led to abandonment of the project in total failure.

There can develop a sense in public sector organisations – and as a seasoned public servant I have seen it on a number of occasions – that the worst can't really happen to them. They tend to assume that the government, certainly in a well-managed western country, can't go broke, so its underpinning guarantees will ensure that no public organisations ultimately can either. The euro crisis has been a vivid reminder that this may not be true in Greece, Spain, Cyprus maybe elsewhere.

While public organisations can't disappear because of total market failure, they can disappear because of a total lack or withdrawal of governmental support. Here's an example.

# NHS University

The NHS University was abolished in July 2005, less than four years after its creation. New organisations took on some of its functions but other functions disappeared and there are no obvious successor bodies. The idea which underpinned it has been buried with its demise.

So what made it an example of total failure? Firstly, objectives. The NHS University was set up with a great fanfare after the 2001 British general election to provide a university-style umbrella for the post-qualification education of the million-plus healthcare workers in England. It had high-level political support and commitment, and it sailed proudly away on that basis with its eyes firmly on the distant horizon of an independent university with its own status and statutes. It was also, by common consent, well funded. It developed as an organisation in a university mould, principally staffed by people with an academic, academic-administrative or medical training background.

It lacked a cohort of managers whose roots were in the provision of healthcare, who understood the needs and the practical imperatives of healthcare, and could win the confidence of healthcare managers by listening to and attending to their needs. Early on, this didn't matter so much, but in a relatively short period a substantial gap emerged between the views of the NHS University about its mission and the critical mass of senior NHS managers, who saw their own immediate problems not addressed despite substantial funding.

When the government's preoccupation moved from expansion and renewed vision to critical scrutiny of public sector expenditure, and a willingness to slaughter sacred cows, the NHS University was reviewed. The conclusion that much of the NHS University was built on sand was highly predictable. So was the recommendation to roll up some of the expensive illusions, and save money. The review was accepted by ministers, and the NHS University moved very quickly from expansion to termination.

The root cause was obvious: the NHS University failed to understand who its real customers were – healthcare organisations rather than politicians – and because of that, it failed to assess and deliver what those customers wanted.

*In extremis*, closure of the business or institution can be the right response: although such cases are rare, sometimes it really is better to let an organisation die and start anew somewhere else. The lessons to be learnt here are about recognising this, knowing when to give up and seeing a lost cause for what it is.

# Shallow failure: the Panama Canal passage

The second major variant of the failure curve, shallow failure, has much wider implications for far more people in more organisations than the Niagara drop, so it is very important to understand. I call the trajectory the Panama Canal passage partly because it looks like a huge canal and partly because the Panama Canal provides a safe, accelerated passage to a ship's destination.

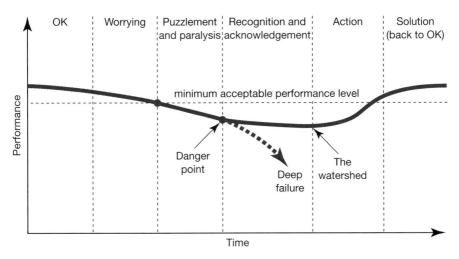

*Shallow failure: the Panama Canal passage*

Shallow failure happens when a company or an organisation is going through a tricky period early in the trajectory of failure, but at a point where people have become aware of this and are trying to deal with it as best they can, in an honest and open way. Performance will have fallen below acceptable levels and so the position will not be sustainable in the long term. But this will have been recognised and there will be a willingness to try and turn things around, so in this case performance and perception of performance do not diverge. Examples of this are harder to find because things haven't gone enormously wrong; they are being put right without a huge furore, and usually keeping out of the headlines. However, here is one from the retail sector.

## Shallow failure at Sainsbury's

The UK grocery chain Sainsbury's fell into this category a few years ago. There were doubts over its market share and the (lack of) differentiation of its brand because 'below' it, principally Tesco, but also others, were increasing market share relentlessly and convincing the public that they were as good as Sainsbury's in the products and services they could offer to the middle of the market. Above them, Waitrose and Marks & Spencer were differentiating themselves by demonstrably offering superior quality and extending their customer base into middle territory by compressing price differentials. But Sainsbury's acted quickly by pushing back just as it had been pushed, downwards to show that its quality was better but its price was comparable, and upwards to show that its quality was comparable but its price was better – and it was a positively distinctive brand. And so it resumed – and continues to this day – its progress as a successful major grocery chain.

The description might also apply to various credit-crunch survivors such as Barclays, HSBC and UBS, though their subsequent problems, described elsewhere in this book, might call that into question. It might also apply to Accenture, which wrote off hundreds of millions of pounds to escape from the onerous NHS IT programme, the biggest civilian IT programme in the world. But it did escape and has carried on successfully elsewhere.

It also applies to the Disney corporation. In early 2012, the Disney corporation recorded a $200 million loss on *John Carter*, a special-effects-laden film based on the Edgar Rice Burroughs book series, making it one of the biggest flops in cinema history. The head of the film studio, Rich Ross, stepped down shortly after. He had taken the job two and a half years previously with a mission to cut costs and develop new hits. But the studio's losses continued despite major restructuring efforts. Ross told staff: 'The best people need to be in the right jobs, in roles they are passionate about, doing work that leverages the full range of their abilities. I no longer believe the chairman role is the right professional fit for me.' Ross had the insight and the honesty to step down at the right time for him and for Disney. The result: Disney moved on quickly and with barely a wobble to its share price: a case of shallow failure.

Three factors are critical to keeping failure shallow and then recovering. They are:

- **The organisational and leadership mindsets.** These will almost certainly have to change because they have failed to keep performance at an acceptable level – simply reinforcing the way things have gone on is unlikely to hold the position, let alone make it better. And, if the mindset of the organisation has to be changed, the mindset of those leading it will have to change first. There is no uniform answer to how it will need to change, but in later chapters I will set out some possibilities.

- **Clear-sightedness about what the problem is.** Not recognising that the problem is a big one will mean it is not given priority and is therefore not addressed or solved. I deal with the positive side of this (i.e. ensuring you give such problems the attention they need) in Chapter 14.

- **Shared ownership of the problem.** A shared approach among all parties who have a capacity to solve the problem, whether or not they were its principal cause, is vital. So, in publicly managed and funded systems and services (or even more widely in partly publicly, partly privately funded ones – see the next example), there are of necessity some arbitrary rules that take the place of market mechanisms. This can on occasion allow a very seductive but destructive tactic when one party manipulates an arbitrary rule in their favour and ensures that the consequences of their decision are all positive for them. They disregard the negative consequences which, if they had analysed them, they would have clearly seen impacting adversely on another party. It isn't even a zero-sum game. One party is getting gain without pain, which it doesn't deserve, and another party is getting loss irrespective of what it does. At its simplest and most common, this gaming ascribes the costs incurred by one party to another party. Typically the injured party knows this is being done but can do nothing about it, which also harms relationships. Roy Lilley in his blog of 12 June 2012 illustrated this beautifully.

## Crossed wires

'Mum is registered disabled and because of her frailty, has a life-line device, made by Tunstall telephones, linked to a call centre someplace, supplied by Surrey Health Borough Council and paid for by me. It only works if the phone-line works.

When the phone-line packed up the call centre didn't know because the type of kit they are using cannot detect a problem with the line. So, it's not their fault. The Tunstall kit is out-moded, they have better kit but it is not in use here. So, it's not their fault.

The Council make it clear they are not responsible in the event of the phone-line packing up. So, it's not their fault. The phone-line is provided by the Post Office. Quaint? Yes. But, remember we are dealing with a 90+year-old and unlike most other pro-viders the PO will still send a bill that can be paid for with a cheque – a USP if you are a customer of a certain age.

The Post Office has a UK based call centre that is process driven and utterly without common-sense. When I tried to report the fault they refused to have anything to do with me as I wasn't the subscriber. They insisted on speaking to Mum and for security and Data Protection purposes, wanted her date of birth … You can imagine Mum's reaction.

The youngster on the phone seemed totally unaware that a disabled person, with a lifeline phone, might merit some form of priority. I had to 'prove' to them Mum was a 'welfare case' and that involved revealing details of her medical conditions. Bang goes the Data Protection Act!

Each day we have checked the progress of the repair. Twice they have promised to call back. I'm still waiting. They are either liars or the call centre phones are provided by the Post Office. Apparently, it is not their fault. It is the fault of Open Reach, their contractors, a BT subsidiary, with no public face.

Open Reach visited and told us what we knew; 'there's nothing wrong with the phone, it's the line'. Since then a bloke came to dig up the lawn, Mum signed the consent form. He sprayed a cross on the grass and went away – never to return. Each day we have had a promise from the Post Office that the phone would be fixed by the end of the day. Incompetent, stupid, inept, hopeless, dissemblers, prevaricators? What?

The latest from the PO? Open Reach's supplier has had his copper wire pinched. You couldn't make it up. It's not the Post Office's fault. It is not Open Reach's fault. It is not the supplier's fault, nor Tunstall, neither the call centre nor the Council.

The Council have risen to the challenge and sent someone in, to make sure Mum is OK, every day! In their own way each of these other organisations is probably competent. But, put them all together and they become useless. Without leadership and common purpose they are bungling and inept. No shared motivation to succeed in the name of the customer because each is the other's customer. Each looking for excuses whilst the real customer is collateral damage.'

So, to stay on the shallow trajectory, the serious problems must be recognised as such, and fresh ways of resolving them must be found.

If that is done, the shallow downsloping will flatten and the business will move into a phase of gentle but steady recovery. If it fails to do this, it will quickly rollercoaster into the deep failure trajectory. The difference between shallow and deep failure is immense and, therefore, what is required to remedy shallow failure and avoid deep failure is very important to all businesses.

One of the key questions in evaluating an organisation, a business or an operating subsidiary and its current wellbeing is whether the organisation and its leadership alone and unaided will succeed in solving the problems they face, or whether some form of external input will be needed, and if so, what form this should take. Naturally, many organisations seek help from time to time to buttress efforts or add skills that are internally lacking. The key is recognition that help is needed and a willingness to take it. This characterises shallow failure. It is the sort of failure that we are all likely to face at some time in our working lives.

But there is a more difficult question for businesses that are facing fundamental problems. Has a point been reached where a different approach (i.e. a different regime) is necessary to achieve change and recovery? This needs to be evaluated and assessed, probably externally to ensure objectivity and a balanced perspective – and the sooner, the better. If that different approach is necessary but doesn't happen, then shallow failure will become deep failure.

# Broadening failure: the Grand Canyon

Failure, centrally deep failure, starts and is identified as specific failure, typically the failure of an enterprise, a business or an organisation. But it may not stop there, and if you are in the middle of it, it is crucial that you watch for this and understand it. It will affect what you can and what you should do. I call it the Grand Canyon for obvious reasons: it still has the characteristics of a Yosemite – a deep, sharp valley that you can crash into – but it is broader, deeper, probably multi-layered, and it needs the most concerted efforts to get out of it.

The Grand Canyon describes a multi-business, multi-organisation or whole-system failure. It should be said that, although a system can

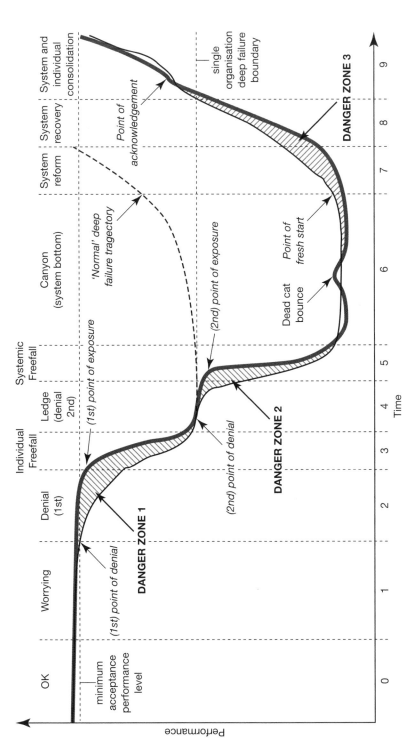

*Broadening failure: the Grand Canyon curve*

experience deep failure on its own rather than always being pushed into it by its constituent organisations and businesses; it could be the *system's* component parts (expressed in the Unbreakable Triangle diagram in Chapter 10) that are not working. To understand the right way forward for a business or organisation in this situation, it is critical to determine whether the failure needs dealing with individually or whether it can only be put right by dealing with the whole system.

Here are some examples of broadening failure:

- The scandal over the deaths of several children receiving heart operations at Bristol, which became public in the late 1990s, surfaced as an issue about practices at the Bristol Royal Infirmary. My sense at the time was that everyone – politicians, the media, the public – had become hysterical about what had happened and were seeing it as a deep failure, not simply at Bristol but of the whole NHS. They were partly right in that it showed something fundamentally wrong across the whole of this huge system, the world's third or fourth largest enterprise; and partly wrong, because it did not show that everything was wrong or that the NHS *as a system* was fundamentally flawed or unworkable. It took some time to work through and come up with the right remedy, to allow the system to move beyond deep failure. This solution involved a complete reframing of acceptable clinical and managerial behaviour: evidenced, with clarity of responsibility, action on concerns, and a requirement to have complete data.

- The furore over phone hacking at the *News of the World* spread similarly, from a concern about rogue behaviour in one paper to an acceptance that the practices of journalists and media organisations generally needed to change, and, following the Leveson Inquiry, would change.

- The revelations about Jimmy Savile moved from what sexual abuse he was guilty of and who knew to the much broader issues of organisational complicity, tolerance, blindness and finally incompetence at the BBC. The initial failure of senior management at the BBC to see these wider issues led to the resignation of its Director-General and plunged the organisation into instant but deep failure.

- The individual bankruptcies and bailouts of the 2008 credit crunch have long since broadened out into an understanding that the faults were industry-wide, cultural and systemic, and needed system-wide action. Two that have continued to rumble on are the industry-wide misselling of payment protection insurance, currently estimated to be likely to cost Lloyds nearly £7 billion and other UK banks a total of over £7 billion; and the LIBOR rate-fixing scandal, which is now implicating many banks.

- The confirmation of Lance Armstrong's drug taking has revealed that he was far from alone, that drug taking was endemic and besmirched the whole sport of cycling, so that the solution relates to the way the whole sport is run and policed, not just individual behaviour.

## To sum up ...

The lessons from the examples presented in this chapter are:

- The context matters: understand it.

- Is it changing? If so, review your approach and realign it to the changed context.

- Is it changing too much and/or too fast? If so, you will need to protect yourself and alert those concerned with that wider context – they could be your bosses, your parent organisation, those who buy from you.

- If it's changing too fast or too much then it may be threatening a much broader failure, and will no longer be solely or principally your (or your organisation's) problem.

- You need to try to ensure there is a common acceptance of this among those (one or many) whose problem it now is.

- Your role should then change from lead problem solver to sharing the problem and supporting the solving process.

To recap the last two chapters, there are three types of failure: shallow, deep and total.

- The first is commonplace and readily remediable with the right approach.

- The second is fundamentally serious but my key message is that this situation too can be rescued. You need to understand how broad it is, in order to work out how best to tackle it.

- It can broaden into whole-system failure. This is more fundamental and needs a different approach. It is vital that you know whether what you are seeing is individual business or whole-system failure. Either way, it can still be put right, albeit with different actions.

- Total failure cannot be remedied. It stands as the ultimate warning.

# part two

# Avoiding failure

*Sometimes I think my most important job as a CEO is to listen for bad news. If you don't act on it ... that's the beginning of the end.*

BILL GATES

Failure doesn't come like a bolt from the blue. In Chapter 2, I explained the slow and corrosive divergence between performance and perception of performance. Once you've seen this happening a few times, you realise that there are repeated symptoms, signals, patterns and behaviours. And they are actually quite easy to detect. The more warning signs you notice, the more you should worry, and the more immediate the need to act.

On the other hand, when you are in the middle of a problem, it is very hard to stand back and take an objective, disinterested view. You are the subject. In addition, fear and self-justification can drive interpretation in a favourable direction.

While you can't make people see who don't want to see, or who have put a protective screen around them, there are things that anyone can look out for and test. These won't be conclusive, but they may give grounds for serious thought about where the organisation or organisations working together stand.

And what about people outside? They are often concerned that they won't be able to see what's really going on – the smokescreen will be much too thick for them. Actually, there usually isn't a cover up. It's a fog in which everyone is lost. Even where there is a smokescreen, it will be incomplete, so the signs will be visible. This will trigger an alarm and the alarm will keep ringing.

So if you are there on the ground or looking in from the outside, how will you see what is going on, and what should you look out for to indicate that things are not OK? Look for six (often overlapping) signs. If you act on what they tell you about the culture of the organisation and the behaviours of its staff, you may be able to help head off impending trouble and move on.

I have divided the six signs into two sets of three. This is a pragmatic, approximate, overlapping division to help provide a framework for identification. But such a classification is always somewhat arbitrary and some of the examples could have been moved elsewhere.

The first three are signals that the business and the people in it are lost, misguided or paralysed. Bad things *will happen or are happening to them*. I call them **passive warning signs**. Chapter 4 describes and analyses them. The second three are **active signs**: signals that the business, the people in it, and their behaviours, are misleading or doing the wrong things. They are *making things happen*, albeit the wrong things. I call these active signals 'alarm bells'. Chapter 5 describes and analyses them.

The six signs of failure are:

- ignorance
- certainty
- complacency
- obsession
- manipulation
- evasion

Finally, in Chapter 6, I look at prevailing, dangerous cultures which may prompt, encourage or allow an organisation to slide into the alarming behaviours I describe in Chapters 4 and 5. Understanding and seeking to alter these cultures, my aim in Chapter 6, is another big part of avoiding failure.

# 4

# Passive warning signs

This chapter focuses on the three 'passive' warning signs: namely, ignorance, certainty and complacency.

## Ignorance

I have frequently found, in failing organisations I have managed and when I have been into organisations in trouble, that no one knows what's actually going on. People may complain about it or they may simply put up with it, but it is amazing that they take so few steps to remedy it. There's almost always an opportunity to get some information, and if you have got bad information, to get better information. Once you start using it, as I show later in the book, things start to improve and you get into a virtuous circle. And it's almost as bad when information is available but is not used, is not valued, and so doesn't make a difference.

One organisation I worked with was having enormous trouble in delivering the volume and type of surgery it needed to deliver, in orthopaedics. But it hadn't worked out what its real capacity was, where it had bottlenecks (shoulders, hips, knees, backs, feet or hands), and so whether this was a single problem or a series of parallel but different ones. It had a lot of good data, enough to work out its inherent capacity. This clearly showed there were plenty of areas where it was performing satisfactorily, but one or two key bottlenecks which could be remedied simply and cheaply.

There are two factors linking information and its proper use. As the above example shows, one is performance management. But there is an even simpler one – communication. Very often, information is there but lies dormant in an organisation. Simply to broadcast it, to spread it, to let people know about it, would make an enormous difference, but so often this is not done. Rogue trader Jérôme Kerviel lost the huge French bank Société Générale $6.3 billion in a few days in early 2008. By not monitoring Kerviel properly, by not obtaining and using information it could have used, the organisation didn't know it was at risk.

As a result it was unable to take the necessary steps to protect itself. It emerged in July 2012 that JPMorgan made losses of $6 billion on massive bets made by Bruno Iksil, known as 'the London Whale' and 'Voldemort' in the London markets (and hence highly visible). These bets were supposed to protect the bank but actually put it more at risk and were not properly scrutinised or monitored. The CEO, Jamie Dimon, said that the episode had 'shaken our company to the core'.

If an organisation is ignorant of what is intrinsically important, nothing is prioritised and you get either the sheer number of demands on staff leading to despair and inaction, or frantic attempts being made to satisfy each demand by running a little way in one direction, and then turning and running in another. This activity is typically fruitless and destroys morale. It happens when people feel overwhelmed: too many things are coming at them, too fast. It creates 'rabbits in the headlights' paralysis.

It is vital to distinguish priorities and to focus on some more than others. An organisation's true priorities will be apparent from what it does and what it focuses on. This is how you can test this:

- Itemise the organisation's current priorities and see how strongly scaled they are, i.e. are there big differences between them or not?

- Does one in particular stand out above all others: for example, getting a new capital investment, flotation, winning more business, expanding the workforce?

- Set out what you think a typical organisation in this position should have as its priorities, given the general environment in which it operates, its general constraints and requirements, plus the local variance upon that which makes every organisation different from any other.

- Once the two lists (yours and the typical organisation's) have been compiled and restricted to a maximum of six items, see if there is a substantial divergence between them, especially at the top of the list.

- If there is, then you have your first warning sign: ignorance.

- A more thorough-going process of reviewing your organisation's current priorities should begin urgently on the basis that something may indeed be amiss.

When I arrived at West Hertfordshire Hospitals, many people were working desperately hard to deal with a lot of problems bearing down on the organisation. They hadn't given up on any of them, but they would run at one problem for a while and then realise that another one was becoming more urgent and so devote their attention to that, then another, and so on. Not surprisingly, few if any of the problems were sorted out and things got worse and worse.

A secondary symptom of ignorance is that managers will have a sense of overburdened agendas. They will be expected to do everything when the only way of sensibly attacking issues is to focus on the most important ones first of all.

## Straw in the wind

A business was in severe difficulties. It didn't have enough money and things seemed to be getting worse. Some staff were leaving and those remaining were being asked to do more and more. Then the business realised it had another priority ... Then it realised it needed to do something quickly elsewhere ... Then it decided it had to make a quick response to a major health and safety alarm ... and so on.

The company did a bit of work on each, but it failed to complete each task, and as it parked each one and turned its attention away, the resistance it faced or had provoked gradually built up until issue by issue a great tide of reaction arose which it was unprepared for and unable to deal with. Staff had developed a siege mentality, and siege it proved to be, as they were gradually overwhelmed and the business went into deep failure.

What this example shows is a lack of follow-through and the absence of an execution culture. In this situation people are passive, not proactive. Passivity is based on a belief that things happen to people and organisations, that everyone and everything is driven by events. This engenders reactive rather than learning behaviours, and what one sees in these situations is repetitive behaviour. People go on and on with the same tactics, even as again and again they fail to produce results. They have stopped believing that they have an alternative, so what else can they do?

Some questions:

- What are the key measures of achievement? In many cases, the answers will be measures that are countable on the fingers of two hands, with even the biggest aggregate figures often being less than 100. So no excuse here.
- Are the board of directors or managers unaware of such simple facts and figures?
- Irrespective of the figures, do they know what is happening, or where?
- Do they know why or is it seen as inexplicable?
- Is basic information passed around, especially to those people and those services that need to perform better?

If the answer to all or even some of these straightforward questions is no, people won't realise what is happening. Ignorance of and lack of insight into basic information will mean inaction on simple, solvable but major concerns. Performance will inevitably stagnate and then deteriorate, leading to major performance failures.

Harold Macmillan famously answered a question about what was important in his UK premiership with the phrase 'Events, my dear boy, events'. In his words lies an important truth for the manager. If we let events determine what we do, we will run around in circles. If we master our response to events, we will be able to manage successfully.

To identify if this warning signal applies, check whether any issues that would be seen as relatively minor elsewhere, capable of being contained or put on the back burner, are taking up a lot of time and energy. If they are, it is almost certain that really big issues will not be receiving the priority they need.

Lack of any performance management is a related problem. An organisation may have the right objectives but no implementation drive.

People do what they can, and if it doesn't work they think they have done their best. They don't work to agreed goals and targets, so there isn't regular feedback within the organisation that things are going wrong, and that something needs to be done.

The purpose of monitoring performance is to check whether performance is going in the right direction. Where performance is not monitored, failures are not noted and nothing is done to correct them. The shortfall in performance turns from marginal to serious, to dramatic, to catastrophic. If it is monitored, small adjustments can put things back on track. The penny will drop. It will be evident which tactics are not working and where new ones – and new skills – are needed. Ask: how does an organisation know whether its performance or the performance of those whom it buys services from is meeting its needs? What indicates that its performance is diverging in a worrying or unacceptable way?

Even if the information needed for monitoring performance is good and widely available, key questions and problems remain:

- Is there agreement about it and a system for using it? If not, it risks being published and then ignored.

- Is the assumption (wrongly) made by everyone that those whom the information directly affects will act on it as needed? If so, no one will act until performance has unequivocally gone wrong.

- At this point several people with different but interrelated and interlocking responsibilities will become alarmed and start to use the information to attempt to manage performance. This will prove to be a confusing duplication.

- It will overburden those who have to effect change, and set in hand contradictory corrective measures.

So performance monitoring alone is not enough. It can tell you what is wrong but you still have to do something about it and for that you need a system of performance management. So ask:

- What is the system of performance management and how does it work?

- Who is responsible for taking action?

- Who is responsible for monitoring it?
- Who ultimately requires the actions to be taken?
- Are there the means to ensure these actions are taken via a single line of accountability?

If these questions cannot be answered simply and convincingly, there is fog and foghorns should be sounding.

# Certainty

In this case, management is so sure that it already knows the answer that it doesn't bother to find out the truth – and so often doesn't even recognise that there is a problem to start with. The managers have an untested self-belief that is strong enough to give them a sense of invulnerability.

Believing that they are better than everyone else, particularly those who serve them, such managers ignore any unwelcome explanations of what is going on. So things are left as they are – and they don't get better, they tend to get worse because what could be done isn't being done and staff aren't being alerted to what they could do. As the counter-evidence of reality builds up, they discount it and seek alternative explanations until finally, too late, it becomes impossible to deny. Worse still, if the conviction about being right is strong enough, they may immunise themselves against alternative and, in many cases, unwelcome explanations of what is going on and attack those who challenge them as disloyal. This is a clear warning signal. It was reported of Fred 'the Shred' Goodwin, the now disgraced CEO of RBS in the time leading up to its crash, that he sacked the risk manager who warned of what was to come.

Because in such cases managers assume they are right, and because in other areas they have a track record of doing well, they don't look for other solutions – and so the problem isn't tackled. People will have risen towards the top of organisations because they have been, or have been perceived to be, good in more junior jobs and this inevitably has the effect of persuading those people that they have capability and judgement. But it does not mean they are necessarily right or will always make the right judgements. If they forget that, they can develop a very dangerous sense that they automatically know best. Others, typically practitioner staff or more junior staff in the organisation, or customers outside it, will be brushed aside.

The *Titanic* could not sink. But it did. IBM, a company that once dwarfed every other in its field with three-quarters of the computer market, was certain that the future of computers lay in large main-frame computing, not in individualised personal computers. So it left Microsoft to write the software for the operating systems for these machines (Windows), only to find that the PC revolution created a market much bigger than the mainframe one. IBM thought it knew the answer already but it didn't.

When you encounter a unit, service or organisation with a major but unresolved problem:

- Be very suspicious when you are told 'we are already doing everything we can'.

- Test the explanations. They will describe the difficulty, the causes, the unimpeachable action and behaviours already in place, and the key means of resolution which circumstances deny them.

- These explanations will be flawed at best, and typically will be wrong.

- Even when they are right, they will normally be missing the point.

- Don't accept them.

- Satisfy yourself.

Money is important, but it is a mistake to see money as everything. In the crisis that gripped the NHS in 2006, when a number of organisa-tions were overspending but the system itself was in balance, there was a panic reaction nationally, which forced component organi-sations to take short-term draconian measures. I knew one such organisation very well. It certainly saved some money in the short term, but in doing so it disempowered staff, corroded systems and damaged services. And it didn't achieve the objective because, at the time when I got to know it, it was deemed to be fundamentally failing – all because it had been trying to achieve one apparently over-riding objective. The lesson here is that the immediate bottom line is not the ultimate determinant of long-term failure or success – and worse, it may act as a veil that conceals impending failure.

## Financial performance isn't everything

The biggest scandal to hit the NHS for some years was at Mid Staffordshire Hospitals where, during a prolonged period between about 2005 and 2008, many patients' needs were ignored or not met, or they were treated in a completely uncaring way. This arose and lay undetected because good financial performance was pursued at practically any (non-financial) price, including acceptable standards of care and dignity. Not only did the hospital not understand what this meant; it escaped the notice of monitors and regulators. Finally it all came out, throwing the hospital into deep failure and subsequently causing convulsions in wider healthcare management and regulation.

Beware of managers – beware of becoming a manager – with a fix-ation on what they must achieve, and of pouring money into black holes. These may be one's own creations and obsessions, such as get-ting a new hospital, or saving essential services for the community, or they may be the requirements or obsessions of others. Not infre-quently these obsessions can be what is seen as precious by staff. While this is a vitally important requirement, it is not the be-all and end-all. An organisation which fails to understand this will run into trouble and end up throwing good money after bad. As the losses pile up, because the losses are seen as inevitable and necessary, nothing is done to stem the flow, and the organisation is precipitated towards failure. So:

- Ask what the driving assumptions and beliefs underpinning the organisation's actions and behaviour are.

- Are they well evidenced? Are they evidenced at all?

- If they are not, then be warned! But don't stop there – that's too negative.

- Seek other explanations yourself. Ask others for them.

- Move the organisation from a confidence that it knows to a determination to find out.

# Complacency

The literature of management shows clearly that most organisations have a limited lifespan of success and that practically none can be successful in an unchanging, enduring way. Even IBM and Marks & Spencer, at the height of their success, saw the world change around them and the source of that success diminish or disappear. The same can be said of politicians. Gordon Brown once said, 'There are two types of politicians: those who get out in time and those who fail.' What would he say about himself?

The requirements in any organisation, for any management, will change from time to time, and the trick is to see that happening. It simply isn't possible to ensure one has the skills in advance to deal with the problem, but if one sees the problem then it is possible to go and look for the necessary skills. The alarm signal is when money is used to compensate for lack of skills, potentially creating a bottomless pit.

I've been involved in helping organisations reduce waiting times and infection from the 'killer' MRSA bug, two completely different tasks. But in both cases, I've seen puzzlement in organisations that don't really know what to do, prompting them finally to respond by throwing money at the problem, in the (partially correct) belief that if enough money is thrown at it, the problem will recede or go away. So patients can be sent to private hospitals for treatment that the NHS hospitals can't deliver in time and many hospitals have isolation facilities and different, more expensive kit and drugs to help combat infection. But the truth is that the practices and habits of relevant staff are actually the key to putting these and so many other issues right. If these practices are not changed, then money will keep being needed and the underlying problem will not be resolved. If they are changed as needed, then less or no extra money will be needed and the problems will be permanently resolved.

So when scanning an organisation that may be running into serious trouble:

- Ask whether some of the long-standing, enduring aspects of the organisation's original vision and approach have the validity they once had. There is no magic rule for how to spot the things that are past their sell-by date.

- Ask what the principal drivers of the organisation's approach and behaviour are.

- Break them down into different parts and understand them on their own terms.

- Is the vision itself still valid? If it is, is the means of achieving it that was chosen still valid?

And what of managers? They typically run into trouble when they think that the skills or ways of working that they have used effectively in the past for different problems will do for a new set of problems. They don't recognise that new skills or ways of doing things are always needed, so they don't learn them and they don't practise them. The result is that problems remain stubbornly unresolved, typically with symptoms of organisational overload – people are working very hard but to little effect and without understanding why.

Ask yourself: do the people in the organisation who need to be skilled and using accepted, state-of-the-art techniques understand them and employ them? If you can't answer this question directly, an indirect indication that this is not happening is the number of 'patch and mend', ad hoc solutions the organisation has adopted, typically involving external assistance.

Managerial grip can disappear without anyone realising. I have seen numerous examples where one or two individuals are playing a crucial part in ensuring that key goals, targets or measures are being met. They act as the performance managers, whether or not they are officially designated so to do. They know what needs to be done to make things happen, the skills they need their staff to have and where they are lacking, and they usually have high personal levels of energy. But the down side is that these are individual efforts rather than system successes, and individuals can leave or move.

Many organisations do reasonably well on key aspects of performance over a sustained period and then, in an equally consistent way, do progressively less well. The deterioration often starts with the disappearance of a key individual from a key position who was buttressing an effort but whose crucial role was not recognised. When he or she goes and is not replaced, the organisation suffers.

The opposite problem is that of a key individual who stays and becomes indispensable. In my experience, many organisations that have got into trouble have become massively over-reliant on one or two Mr or Mrs Fix-Its. These people continue to cope, whatever the situation, providing reassurance and comfort that things are being dealt with properly, but they will probably be creatures of a defective system, which they won't recognise. It is easy to see them as part of the solution when in fact they are much more frequently part of the problem. And it is particularly hard to spot them because they are typically competent and well-motivated people, but often competent in the wrong thing and motivated to avoid opening up the difficulties that simply have to be opened up.

## Responding to the internet revolution

The revolution created by internet opportunities is an example of why organisations and businesses need to be ready to change the way in which they work. Look at who has started internet businesses to support them and who hasn't. A little over a decade ago Waterstones was a great innovative success in bringing modern bookselling methods to the UK and elsewhere. But it did not set up its online business until quite late, by which time Amazon had created a huge business selling books, and everything else, via the internet. Waterstones has recently been struggling to survive, and Borders in the UK has gone. In terms of recorded music, the HMV chain has been very adversely affected by the move to internet downloading, which it hasn't benefitted from. Comet, the electrical retailer, is another casualty, going into administration in November 2012, unlike Dixons, which has connected online more effectively.

In the 1950s and 1960s the dominant American car makers assumed they would remain so. They failed to learn the lessons from their Japanese competitors, who developed and then refined a much more efficient way of building cars. Not until the 1980s and 1990s, when they had competitors as or more powerful than themselves, did the Americans adopt these lean methods. But it was too late. The need to (temporarily) nationalise General Motors after the 2008 credit crunch shows the consequences.

## To sum up ...

Beware of managerial behaviours and approaches based on ignorance, certainty and complacency. If you see them, try to alert who you can, and try to do what you can. The perceptions underlying them will, sooner or later, diverge markedly from reality and, however passively, precipitate failure.

The antidotes to these three approaches are described in Part 4 of this book: in particular, for ignorance, see Chapter 11 (information: nourishment for managers); for certainty, see Chapters 12 (especially the sections on living with and loving imperfection, and on managing the unknown) and 13 (gauging the environment); and for complacency, see Chapters 9 (especially the section on relentless management) and 10 (especially the sections on passivity and risk management).

# 5

# Active alarm bells

In this chapter I will look at the three warning signs that things are 'actively going wrong' and are speeding the business towards failure: obsession, manipulation and evasion.

## Obsession

If an organisation or its leadership is obsessively pursuing a single goal, at the expense of others, this is likely to be dangerous because the goals it is neglecting or downgrading will remain important. Moreover, the fact that the latter might be more important than the chosen goal will not be realised, even when it is clearly true. This typically happens because the chosen goal is seen as an unquestionable good, something that people can commit themselves wholeheartedly to, whereas each and every goal needs to be scaled against feasibility, affordability and price – in a monetary but even more importantly in a non-monetary sense. The obsession could be building a new hospital, school or road, setting up a new business or launching a takeover, irrespective of the critical circumstances surrounding it.

### White elephants and architectural monuments

In the public sector, the obsessive pursuit of a new facility at the expense of virtually everything else is all too common. There are many instances of theatres, opera houses and sports facilities being built without adequate funds being available to pay for and run them, so throwing the organisations responsible for them into fundamental crisis. London's Royal Opera House and Sadler's Wells Theatre are wonderful architectural monuments, but the final (excessive) costs of both plunged the organisations that commissioned them into financial failure. More recently, the costs of the new Leicester Haymarket Theatre, the Curve designed by the world-famous Uruguayan architect Rafael Viñoly, rocketed from £26 million to over £60 million, pushing that theatre into failure. In each case a great architectural monument became the end goal, and the fact that it wasn't affordable was forgotten.

An obsessive pursuit of growth or market share, as with Northern Rock, or an ambitious, prestigious project, like the A380 Airbus, should also trigger this alarm bell. Conversely, it could mean trying to keep a service or line of business that has actually become very problematic and should be let go.

When Marks & Spencer ran into trouble a few years ago, as we saw in Chapter 2, it was still trying to keep long-term loss-making businesses going abroad, notably in France and Belgium. It wrongly thought that it needed the international repute such businesses brought. Getting rid of them and focusing on the overwhelmingly important domestic business was part of putting things right.

In June 2012, after ploughing more than £250 million and a decade's effort into getting into Japan, Tesco sold 50% of its stake in over 100 stores there for the token sum of ¥1 and paid the rival Japanese supermarket Aeon a £40 million dowry to take its loss making chain off its hands. In announcing this, Tesco said that it meant it would have 'no further financial exposure to the Japanese business or its operations'. As Kantar Retail analyst Bryan Roberts said, 'Without some serious mergers and acquisitions, Tesco were never going to reach the scale required to create a profitable business in what remains one of the most competitive markets on earth.' But Tesco did the right thing and so kept failure shallow.

## Rationalisation in a health authority

In a hospital group I knew, the chief executive and board became convinced that the right way forward was rationalisation of services between two existing hospitals that were fairly close to each other. Neither was felt to be big enough to provide the full range of services safely or economically, though in such cases it is usually a matter of degree and judgement rather than an issue of absolute safety or economy.

The proposed solution was to put some services in one hospital and some in another, which meant taking some services away from both.

The opposition to losing services (despite the gains) proved particularly intractable and difficult, and management struggled increasingly to get the better of it, spending more and more time and energy in doing so, and in both cases failing. That focus of attention had other very negative consequences. The organisation started to run into major trouble in reducing waiting times, as it was required to do nationally. It didn't focus on this as much as the rationalisation, and it didn't apply the necessary level of analysis and practical skill in redesign as a result.

And beware! The obsessive fighting for a cause is not just a trap for dreamers, those who see the beautiful new facility as solving all problems. It can also be a trap for dreaming realists. They are the ones who 'know' that the current state of things can't go on, that there has to be rationalisation, modernisation and reorganisation. They can forget another stubborn reality: the inertia and refusal to change that exist in stable long-term situations – an insight behind the phrase, 'If it ain't broke, don't fix it.' (Ideas in Chapter 9 takes this forward.)

Trusting 'never, never' promises sets off the same alarm. This is when strategy is based upon some seemingly worthwhile or deserved 'end' which is inherently uncertain. It requires this 'end' (e.g. resource, buildings, business) to be delivered in the future. But those, typically *outside* the operating unit or the organisation, who are supposed to deliver it or make it happen, have not actually committed or promised to do so and the commitment has not been checked, often because of the unconscious fear that the answer will be no. They may simply not see it as a priority or something they wish to do, so relying on the assumed commitment is simply living on borrowed time.

Even if it's not declared, almost every organisation has a vision of the future as they want it to be, and as they think it should be. If it's not explicit, it still informs their view of how they proceed, what they want to happen and how they wish to cope. It may be quite a low-key, pedestrian vision or it may relate to a future that is very different from the present. But the real point is that having a vision does not make it a reality, particularly if the vision includes a number of features that are not within the control of the organisation. When people come to rely on their vision, take it for granted and assume that it either is or will be reality, then they are heading for the rocks.

An organisation is boxing itself into a corner if it needs a particular version of reality to come true to make it viable. In most cases there is little reason to think that this will happen, or at the very least happen exactly as is wished. If some aspects of that reality happen, but others do not, the likelihood is that it will be more of a nightmare than a panacea. So once one moves into a position of relying on something that is only one possible outcome, then one is moved into the realms of failure. The organisation has become passive and complacent and is not using the means available to cope, to survive and to thrive.

A very important, extreme version of this is a refusal to accept a doomsday scenario, with claims such as 'They can't shut us down, we're too important', or 'Someone will come to our rescue, our assets are really precious'. But look at the examples. No one came to the rescue of Barings Bank or the NHS University: cases of total failure.

People and organisations can get hooked on what to someone at some time seemed a good idea, without really evaluating whether it ever was, or still is, a good idea. In these cases people may have responded to a change in the climate or in what looks like government policy or national requirements, and committed themselves to a direction which involved outlaying substantial sums of money. The policy requirement or government initiative then turns out not to mean quite what it was thought to have meant, or not infrequently the government changes its mind. But the organisation, having committed itself so far, does not go back and limit the original mistake. It compounds it because it fears to look back and say it was wrong.

The lesson: always have an alternative, a trap door to escape through, a plan B.

# Manipulation

This is about inaccurate reporting. It could be what former UK Cabinet Secretary Sir Robert Armstrong famously described as being 'economical with the truth' – reporting only what you have to and not giving a full picture. Or it could be 'turning a blind eye' – seeing some information but choosing not to report it. Inaccurate reporting does not necessarily lead to total falsehood and failure, but it is a slippery slope and, once an organisation is on it, it is easy to keep sliding. My own experience at the Royal United Hospital, Bath, was of taking over a hospital where waiting lists had been hidden, waiting times underreported and a thoroughly misleading impression of compliance given when waits were in truth long and frequent.

This sort of glossing over can start as a short-term fix, used to carry an organisation through until it can solve a bigger problem. The most obvious example of this is borrowing. One piece of borrowing is justified to get the organisation out of a temporary difficulty; but then if a second loan is used to underpin the first and a third to underpin the second then the organisation is left in an increasingly false position. That is how Nick Leeson started at Barings Bank in the 1990s. It's how Société Générale got caught out with Jérôme Kerviel in 2008, and even more recently UBS with Kweku Adoboli in September 2011. The danger is that the organisation becomes reliant on such fixes until eventually reporting standards and good accountancy practice are left behind.

In a crisis, managers in many organisations use any means necessary to keep afloat, and this is reasonable as long as they understand what they are doing and see it as a temporary expedient. The problem becomes a potential cause of failure when it is done as a matter of routine and people are unable to see it as masking their true position. In the NHS a few years ago, it became widespread practice to borrow money from other areas, only to return it just after the end of the accounting period or not at all, with the effect that investment in infrastructure was sacrificed to ensure that the bottom line was all right. Doing this once might be acceptable, but doing it year after year, as has happened in some places, means a degradation of the infrastructure with risks to continuity and safety. This can precipitate failure, particularly when time runs out on the short-term fix and the underlying problem is exposed.

Be suspicious of an organisation that looks to be heading into deep trouble, then all of a sudden miraculously manages to avoid it. Remember that the rabbit that was pulled out of the hat was secreted somewhere else before. It's sleight of hand. If you see this, be wary and be worried. Look out for what the real underlying position is, where the rabbit came from and what enduring impact pulling it out of the hat will have on the organisation's health, be it financial or otherwise.

When you are looking at an overall financial position:

- Watch out for conveniently balancing items, items which 'just happen' to make things add up. They are usually an optimistic fiction, and are also quite often designed to obscure and deceive.

- If it looks as though an organisation has a problem but one way or another it comes out in balance, ask why.

- Ask where the money came from and whether it should have come from there: if you don't, in due course, someone else is likely to.

### Customer service at Southern Water

According to its regulator, Ofwat, the utility company Southern Water was guilty of misrepresenting customer service performance and failing to make guaranteed service payments to customers who were entitled to them. It was fined £20.3 million by Ofwat, which explained: 'The magnitude of this fine reflects the magnitude of the offence – deliberately misleading the regulator, failure of the Southern Water board of directors to pick up the deception, the resulting poor service to customers and damage to the regulatory regime in general.'

Lines of behaviour are there to ensure probity, honesty and accuracy, and it is really important not to cross them. Where they appear to have been crossed, it is vital to check out whether that was intentional or accidental, and permanent or temporary, and to ensure it does not become ingrained behaviour. If it goes unchallenged, all too often it is compounded and the organisation moves from an accurate account of its position to one that is increasingly false and distorted. Awful things happen after that.

# Evasion

This alarm bell relates to the system in which management works. The over-riding issue is that the separate players in the system cease to work together cohesively or in a mutually supportive way. What drives them is fear – fear of being caught up in the maelstrom – whereas the right attitude is that a problem shared is a problem reduced and an insoluble problem made soluble. That right attitude also involves acknowledging that leaving an organisation to go under will in due course not save you but drag you under as well, because you are part of that system of working.

A system is in trouble when each organisation is making decisions entirely on its own, seeking to maximise its own achievements irrespective of the effect on others. It is set out in terms of its individual impact in Roy Lilley's story of his mother (see page 46).

The turmoil of the British nuclear clean-up industry in July 2008 – when £400 million had to be pumped into the Nuclear Decommissioning Authority (NDA) and total clean-up costs rose by £10 billion in a year – is an example of mutually dependent organisations acting for individual rather than collective benefit. This sorry tale is described in a report by the Department for Business Enterprise and Regulatory Reform (BERR) posted on a government website. Among the failings that the report reveals are the Treasury being at cross-purposes with the NDA and key misunderstandings between the parties involved. If only everyone had worked together and shared responsibility!

An organisation or department can experience a particular difficulty and come under extreme pressure to sort itself out. Linked organisations are relieved at seeing the spotlight shine on another's failure, and seek not to be associated with it. They play a game of musical chairs because they know they will be sitting down as the music stops. The effect is to load increasingly heavy burdens on the one that is in trouble, so weakening its decision-making processes and restricting its chances of sorting itself out. Then musical chairs changes to a game of dominoes, as the failure of one organisation or department pushes the next into difficulty, and the next.

## Lack of coordination in the rail industry

The partners in the UK railway system include not just the train companies but also Network Rail, which manages the equipment and stations, and the government with its transport policy. All too frequently when something goes wrong – trains run late, fares are too high, passengers are dissatisfied – each blames the other. By not supporting each other and not working together, the partners have created a railway system that is fractured and over-complicated, and so doesn't work properly.

As with a single organisation having no priorities, so it is with separate organisations needing to work together. Joint decisions are not taken and joint agreements are not made. The future 'happens' instead of being shaped. This is **default-ual** decision making. If people don't make decisions then a line of least resistance decision happens. Those running away from the problem hope that this will keep them out of trouble. The reverse is almost certain to be true. Leave decision making to chance, let things happen, and you will almost certainly end up with the wrong decision.

To do an objective check:

- See whether partner organisations are sharing goals and difficulties rather than retreating into their corners or 'passing the parcel'.

- If they are doing the latter, bring this out.

- Show people that this is a 'beggar my neighbour' approach.

- Show the consequences for all of them of carrying on in this way and try to engender different behaviours.

Even if you have a good idea, don't assume that your partners will automatically go with it. Remember you have to keep on earning and re-earning credibility. You won't always get it right, but if you get it right enough and you are honest about what you get wrong then the message will get through.

Another variant of evasion occurs when everyone in a system colludes to ignore a problem they're too frightened to acknowledge or tackle. This is usually done by blaming intractable external factors, forces and rules. But it breeds a particularly damaging form of inaction. It leads people to carry on as they are because they don't know what will happen if they change course, even though their current course is ultimately doomed.

## Gridlock in treatment of the elderly

Many elderly patients who come into hospital as emergencies are successfully treated but then need support in the community or nursing home care. The hospital is paid per case and wants to move the patient on as soon as their acute episode is over. But receiving organisations are paid an annual grant irrespective of how many patients they take, and are afraid that such patients will be given to them prematurely or inappropriately. The result: patients remain in hospital longer than necessary without receiving rehabilitative treatment, even though the ultimate cost of caring for them is higher than if they had been moved on. This is because while it costs one organisation, it saves another.

The right approach is to see how the maximum benefit can be given to the patient and how incentives can be aligned so that costs and benefits are shared between organisations. This requires an active approach and cooperation between linked organisations that have genuinely shared interests, but which are currently engaged in unacknowledged and ultimately sterile competition.

Systems that are spending too much money recurrently, trying to do too many things, tend to tackle over-stretch or over-commitment by a series of salami slicing exercises. A more radical but often necessary approach involves saying that some things should be preserved and even enhanced, while others need to be reduced, or eliminated. The latter are often things which are popular and long established and/or which no one has dared to think of doing something about.

Part of the running away occurs when the monitors in a system or parent company exercise insufficient or negligent oversight. This may be because they are too frightened to face up to reality, they hope the problem may go away, they accept explanations that rigorous analysis would knock over, or they simply have poor information and poor checking systems. This means that burgeoning failure goes unchecked, signs of problems are not realised, explanations are not sought and tactics and behaviours that are not delivering can carry on.

So, ask:

- Is the way things are going sustainable? And if the answer is no ...

- Has any organisation set out a credible alternative that will alter the course to an acceptable one?

- Have they started to implement it?

## To sum up ...

Active behaviours to shape, alter and control managerial action, involving a first focus on controlling perception, will inevitably lead to perception and reality drifting apart, and then, sooner or later, to a plunge into failure. The same tactics apply as for the passive warning signs: identify, bring out, take action. But here, because the tactics are active, you may need to be operating outside of the organisation to be effective.

And the antidotes? For obsession, see Chapter 9 (in particular, processing and feedback loops, and imperfect management) and the whole of Chapter 14 (The attentive manager). For manipulation and evasion, the whole of Chapter 10 (the importance of being honest) is key. Equally important is the 'adaptive' management approach and the five key ideas which I set out in Chapter 9.

6

# The cultural litmus test

When alarm bells start ringing, look at the prevailing culture. Is it passive, unquestioning, timid, fearful, unreflective and rigid, or is it inquisitive, open, forgiving, reflective, permissive and flexible? If the first set of words seems more apt, a problem is likely to be bottled up there. Here are some cultural approaches to watch out for, and some suggestions about your response.

## A reckless culture

If a business takes for granted its ability to do what it wants to do, to succeed where it wishes, because it has had previous success, it may plunge into trouble when things don't work out exactly as planned. Here are five examples:

- In March 2011, the Financial Services Authority reported on the collapse of HBOS in the wake of the 2008 credit crunch, saying that HBOS ignored warnings from its internal risk officials and external auditor KPMG. It breached rules requiring banks to put in place adequate risk management systems which would have prevented the disaster: 'HBOS is accused of a reckless culture of lending, continuing to make hugely risky loans even as rivals pulled back as the meltdown loomed.'

- The disastrously chaotic opening of Terminal 5 at Heathrow is another instance of this sort of blinkered, 'carry on regardless' culture.

- In 2007 RBS led a successful hostile takeover of the Dutch bank ABN AMRO costing over £70 billion, most of which was lost by the time of the credit crunch in 2008, and was instrumental in causing the collapse of RBS that year. Commenting on an FSA investigation into the takeover in late 2011, a report in the Guardian said:

  *The board wasn't thinking in any meaningful sense. The directors ... relied for their due diligence on two lever arch folders and a CD. Extraordinary ... Let's get this clear: the hostile takeover of NatWest in 1999 yielded pleasant surprises so the board therefore believed that all hostile takeovers yield pleasant surprises. A six-year-old could spot the flaw in that logic ... How did such a culture of complacency come about?... The non-executives appear to have swallowed whole the view that RBS primarily should be pursuing growth in revenue and profits. Fundamentals of banking – such as a focus on risk, liquidity and capital – became secondary.*

- At the inquest in July 2012 into the death of 22-year-old Kane Gorny in St George's Hospital, south London, from 'dehydration, contributed to by neglect', the Deputy Coroner, Dr Shirley Radcliffe, said that 'a cascade of individual failures had led to an incredibly tragic outcome'. Gorny was so desperate for water he phoned police for help and was not given vital medication to help him retain fluids. Dr Radcliffe described medical staff as being 'blinkered' by Kane's previous behavioural problems and commented that 'Kane was let down by poor communication, lack of leadership ... and a culture of assumption.'

- On 26 October 2012 at Southwark Crown Court, Kweku Adoboli defended himself against charges of gambling away $1.5 billion of his employer, UBS's, money as follows: 'Our book was massive. A tiny mistake led to huge losses. We were these two kids trying to make it work. There was a total of 30 months in trading [experience] between the two of us [Adoboli, 27, and Hughes, 24] in charge of a $50 billion book. We were just losing so much money. It was mental.'

So, ask yourself:

- What is really unforeseen?

- Am I hearing things like this?

    - 'I should have seen that coming'
    - 'I have been saying this for a long time but ...'
    - 'I thought we fixed it last time it happened'
    - 'That was lucky'

Remember:

- Individually, each near miss is an inconvenience or nuisance.
- Sooner or later they will coalesce or line up.
- They will precipitate a headline failure event when they do.
- Near misses are cheap data points – understand them or perish.

# A culture of false reassurance

Businesses which don't enable their staff to articulate problems and which are 'issue' averse are unlikely to come up with real and enduring solutions. Let me give a personal example.

## Medway Hospital

Having noticed on my arrival that Medway Hospital was not particularly clean or cared for, I started to ask questions about health and safety, essential maintenance and the general infrastructure of the hospital. The answers I got were designed to reassure, but my sense was that health and safety issues and the repair and maintenance of infrastructure were under-invested in and under-regarded.

I was then told we were due to have a health and safety inspection and that there was nothing to worry about. I asked for a blow-by-blow analysis of the detailed items we were going to be inspected on. Had I not asked for it, the people involved would simply have muddled through and waited for the health and safety inspector to declare the hospital unsafe. The audit showed a tremendous range of gaps, defects and deficiencies, so we drew up an action plan to put these right one by one, assigning responsibility to named individuals and making it clear that they were accountable for delivery. This approach surprised nearly all the staff involved. I was told repeatedly that they were not used to this approach, that in the past when they had raised issues about investing in health and safety they had been

▶

told there was no money and they would have to do the best they could. I was shown proposals for improvement that had been rejected.

I decided that not only was a new approach needed, but that that new approach needed to be shouted from the rooftops of the hospital. In response to the expressed view that people had been told to get on and shut up, I said that from now on I expected the hospital and its infrastructure to be healthy, safe, secure and properly maintained. If there were actual or potential dangers, I required such matters to be brought out and dealt with. I also made it clear that, where investment was essential to provide and maintain safety, then I would ensure it was provided. This message went round the organisation and was very significant in signalling a basic change in regime and culture.

We worked on the action plan to improve health and safety issues, but I still had nagging doubts that the attitude, culture and expectations hadn't changed sufficiently. I therefore decided to bring in an external health and safety expert to do a completely independent audit. His report was dramatically critical, but proved the final necessary eye-opener for staff, who were now working to change the previous habits and culture of the organisation, showing them how far they had to go. We worked desperately hard for the next two months to meet the defects identified by the external expert.

When the health and safety inspectors came, I insisted we were completely open with them about what we had found, what we were trying to do and what we had not yet done. They totally endorsed the criticisms our external expert had made but at the same time saw that we were actively addressing them. On that basis they gave us a relatively positive report, but to underline the fact that we had not achieved it all, accompanied it with three improvement notices in nine major areas, giving us three months in each case to do the necessary extra work. This was just the right result. It showed that we had moved forward but weren't out of the woods. Three months later, after we had submitted the evidence to them, they lifted the notices. Had we not gone along this difficult and detailed road, I believe we would had been subject to multiple health and safety prosecutions, massive adverse publicity, short-term defensive action that would have been costly and inefficient, and general turmoil across the hospital to add to the huge amount that it had already experienced.

The lessons from this example are as follows:

- Dig, find out for yourself, ensure that no stone is unturned.
- If there are problems, bring them out. Don't be lulled into a false sense of security.
- Confession is not only good for the soul; it's good for the running of the organisation.

# A culture of gaming

This refers to an acceptance, tacit or overt, of tactics and behaviours which seek to push a business or organisation's benefit to any limit that can be got away with. It means rules are interpreted as obstacles or barriers, which it is perfectly fine to push, bend or even dodge round.

## The case of Barclays

Giving evidence to the House of Commons Treasury Select Committee in July 2012, Andrew Bailey, head of the Prudential Business Unit at the UK Financial Services Authority (FSA), said the regulator's relationship with Barclays had become strained in the period immediately prior to the FSA's enforcement action in relation to the fixing of LIBOR rates: 'I felt Barclays was trying it on. There was a culture of gaming, and gaming us. It had to change. We drew the conclusion that there was a problem with this institution; you could not escape the conclusion that the culture of this institution was coming from the top.' The chair, CEO and COO of Barclays all resigned. Barclays was also one of several banks which were found to have engaged in mis-selling of payment protection insurance to the benefit of all those banks at the expense of their customers. As recently as November 2012, the US Federal Energy Regulatory Commission claimed Barclays and four of its traders had consistently rigged the Californian electricity markets between 2006 and 2008, and fined the company $490 million. It should be said that at the time of writing, Barclays has said it will vigorously defend itself against the charge.

In a gaming culture, the desired outcome shifts from ensuring that a customer or patient is satisfied to 'getting away with it' to your advantage. This clearly brings short-term benefits, as you are playing by a different interpretation of the rules from everyone else, but when it does catch up with you, as it almost certainly will, then failure will follow:

- In my own area of healthcare there have been a series of scandals based on highly dubious accounts of how short waiting times were in particular hospitals, when on any normal interpretation they were unacceptably long. At Mid Staffs, management sought to satisfy external regulators about standards, while ignoring the fact that care was shockingly wanting in basic ways. This inevitably caught up with them, creating one of the NHS's biggest ever scandals.

- The very widespread misselling of payment protection insurance by a number of UK banks was based on deliberate, excessive charging of unsuspecting customers, coupled with a collusive approach that allowed bank after bank to do it.

- In professional cycling, the widespread use of drugs by competitors was based on pushing boundaries beyond where they should be and on falsifying what personal success is.

If you suspect such a culture exists, ask:

- What sort of tactics are used here?
- What principles underlie them?
- Are they defensible to customers and the public at large? If not, they need to change.

# A culture of control

A controlling leadership will often have intelligence about the organisation (i.e. it will be able to see what is going on), but it may not share what it sees and what it thinks with the organisation from which it is garnering its intelligence. This is particularly likely where formal structure is unimportant and unclear, and where real power is exercised through personal influence and status as a member of an inner circle or coterie. Those outside the coterie feel they are disempowered and they are likely not to sign up to the objectives or to offer the insights they have into solving the organisation's problems. I have seen the after-effects of such a culture more than once in failing organisations that I have been asked to help. The sense in those situations is that of a spider's web after the spider has gone. Promises, understandings and assumptions: all prove to be shakily based and fall apart.

Given that there are likely to be invisible but very real barriers in such organisations, a very important issue to assess is who moves across the organisation freely. If the answer is everyone and this is the norm, then things are working well and openly. If there are only one or two people who feel free to report upwards and to gather intelligence downwards then there will be a real problem. Most staff will be and will feel disempowered. The organisation will be massively over-dependent on one or two people's insight. It will be biased towards what they have come to believe is possible and will probably reflect where the organisation now is.

If you look hard enough, it will be possible to see how an organisation works and who relates to whom. But even more revealing is how these relationships take place:

- Is top management interested in what staff feel and say or does it separate itself, however subconsciously?

- Is there an approach that 'we decide and they do, and we don't want feedback'? All organisations will pass messages around in some form or other, but are they received; are they heard; are they given real attention?

## To sum up ...

The last three chapters show that, if you want to avoid failure, it is vital to pick up warning signs, passive or active, and to identify a negative or corrosive culture. When you know what to look for, they are pretty easy to spot; they overlap and sadly they can easily multiply. If they remain unaddressed, they will precipitate the organisation's fall into deep failure. If you see them, you can do something about them or at least alert others. As Timothy Geithner, US Treasury Secretary, said: 'This has a classic dynamic that the longer you wait, the harder it is to solve.'

However, after failure has happened, identifying what the warning signs and culture were will help whoever has to put things right. Being catapulted into overt failure because others have finally heard the alarm bells doesn't stop the alarm bells ringing. You still have to put out the fire or catch the thieves. You have to alter the behaviours that triggered them.

In the next part, I will look at how you respond when you are faced with deep 'exposed' failure and how you start to put things right.

# part three

# Curing failure

*A leader is a dealer in hope.* NAPOLEON

As failure is so frequent, so widespread, so inevitably a part of our everyday working lives and experience, no book about it could reasonably claim to have examined the subject thoroughly without going through actual failure and how you deal with it. This is what I do in Part 3. Failure is about businesses, organisations and institutions, but above all it is about people.

At the end of October 2012, the British Broadcasting Corporation was teetering on the edge of failure. Why? Because people had lost confidence in how it had dealt or not dealt with the now exposed sexual abuser, Jimmy Savile. The crucial terms in this firestorm were confidence, honesty, trust, reputation, passivity, collusion, responsibility and action. The BBC's Chairman, Lord Patten, told the *Mail on Sunday* on 28 October 2012, 'The BBC must tell the truth and face up to the truth about itself, however terrible.' So, there was a need for truthfulness within the organisation and for a true account to be given outside, to its audience and to the public generally, who are also its paymasters.

That is why this part of the book starts, in Chapter 7, by looking at communication as the first step towards getting out of failure. It covers internal and external needs, what has to be said, when and how, and describes a sequence of approaches that start in crisis and conclude when reputation is fully restored, usually quite some time in the future.

Nowhere are saying and doing so intimately connected as they are in dealing with and getting out of failure. For those who have to deal with it, being who they say they are, telling everything, doing what they say they are going to do, showing they care, showing they understand the feelings of those who feel they have been failed – and being right! – are all crucial. Saying and doing go together, but at the end of the day it is the doing, the manager's task, that changes things.

In Chapter 8, I go through the next steps that must be taken, beginning with finding out what is really at the root of the problem, partly obvious and usually the material of umpteen opinions, but usually partly concealed and in need of unearthing. Required next is injecting a sense of doing things, action, a sense that problems can be solved. However small the achievement, an achievement nonetheless it will be and will be seen to be. Two comments of Winston Churchill come to mind here. Firstly, he said, 'Success consists of going from failure to failure without losing enthusiasm,' and secondly, 'Before Alamein we never had a victory. After Alamein, we never had a defeat.' To paraphrase, first, you have to keep going, and, second, individual successes need to be turned into structural, systematic successes. To achieve that in business, the processes which drive a business must be revivified and, where necessary, redrawn. By this time, the recovering organisation will be working not just effectively but with the exceptional momentum that was needed to move out of failure. It is critical not to lose this momentum, but to reinforce it so that the business or organisation doesn't halt at average but continues to progress inexorably towards outstanding performance across the board. I conclude Chapter 8 and Part 3 by showing how you can do this.

More than in any other part of the book, in order to convey the immediacy, vividness and detail of what it feels like, I have drawn heavily on my personal experiences. I have been through this three times directly – at Medway, Bath and West Hertfordshire hospitals – as the person coming in to try and sort things out; as an involved but innocent observer several times indirectly, reviewing troubled organisations; and once (after I had been in Medway for a while) as the 'victim' when government ministers decided wrongly that I was part of the problem not its solution. Not surprisingly, these stories remain vivid to me because I was personally involved and, equally unsurprisingly, the one that is most vivid is the one where I was highlighted for blame and opprobrium, where I experienced and had to cope with that.

The assumption in this part of the book is that those sorting the problem out once there is deep failure will be 'new', either to the organisation or at least to the task. The reason for this is twofold. Those close to and high up in the organisation will find it very difficult, first, to survive. But, even if they do, the nearer they were to the key problem or root cause (that they failed to see), the harder they will find it to be objective and to be seen to be capable of sorting things out. That is why in this situation a fresh pair of eyes is normally needed. At the BBC, after the Savile revelations, the relatively new but internally appointed Director-General, George Entwistle, and perhaps others, were in this position. This may explain why the non-executive Chairman, Lord Patten, himself new to his post and to the BBC, gave the initial decisive lead. Much the same had happened in each of the three failing organisations I came into. But in all of these cases and elsewhere, the lead in implementing a solution, in establishing recovery, must be executive. The next two chapters will describe what it means to take that lead.

# 7

# Regaining confidence

At the point at which failure is acknowledged by all, blame and finger pointing will be rife. Those left or brought in to revive things must take some immediate steps. This chapter is written in the form of a guide to such people, because they will inevitably be the ones required to act, but hopefully it will provide general insight to all who are affected by and want to understand this.

## Talking to staff

The first priority is to revive internal communication to demoralised or indifferent staff. That means communicating immediately, widely and fully, and setting up mechanisms to make good communication the norm. In these situations staff have a massive appetite for knowledge and question hard to see what is going on. They want a frank response. It is usually what they suspected and often not as bad as they had feared. On top of the next page you can see the Yosemite curve again, viewed from a communication viewpoint.

Those now charged with putting the organisation and its performance right need to get across that things are going to be different. For this chapter and the next, to make my account more immediate and visceral, I will call 'those' people 'you'. Think of them as you as you read it. Here are the four 'whats' and 'hows' that they – you – will need to say and do:

### 1. OPEN UP WITH A BLITZ OF FACE-TO-FACE, INTERACTIVE COMMUNICATION

Communicate until you are exhausted – using every means at your disposal. It is vital that much of this is face-to-face and interactive. People need to be told the truth and they need to have a chance to query it. Make transparency and honesty your watchwords. Openness, inclusion and conveying a sense of doing something will get you off to a flying start. They raise morale, by convincing people that they are being told

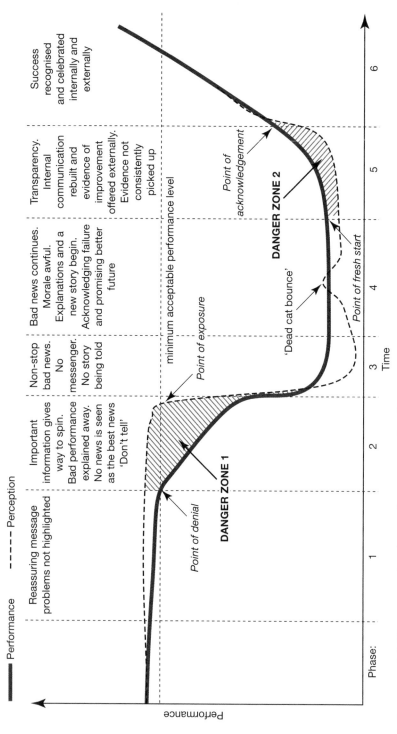

*Trajectory of failing organisations: the communication story*

what is going on and that they are important enough to be told. Here are some tips on how:

- Design timings to maximise who can come to any meetings.

- Differentiate groups with specific interests, influence and concerns, and show you are sensitive to them.

- Explain how you fit in, and the current very difficult circumstances as you see them.

- Set out the positive things that have been done recently.

- Your underlying message must start with the need for honesty and openness and that means baring yourself to a lot of scrutiny. It will come in thick and fast.

- People will want to know your motivation, why you have been brought in and what you think of specific issues. They will want to vent their cynicism that the new will be like the old, with the real 'workers' just getting on with it.

- Tackle the concerns head on, answer every question you possibly can but don't pretend to have answers to questions when you haven't.

- Don't restrict or time-limit questioning.

- Give those too slow or too intimidated to ask questions in meetings the opportunity to do so individually.

Even though it won't be expressed directly, there will be a sense of deep depression, of a crisis that just seems to go on and on, of there being no way out of the conundrum, and staff feeling they have been doing their best but that things are hopeless. So people will hugely appreciate your openness and honesty and the possibility that there is a way forward. Someone is talking to them, opening up to them, sharing the problems and asking them to share the solutions. You will definitely not be saying either that there are no problems or that the problems are insoluble. But they want to feel that the ship is no longer the *Marie Céleste*. In one hospital I told staff that a newly opened facility was not just suffering from the teething troubles that had previously been reported; it was a disaster. 'Oh, we knew that,' they replied. 'Thank goodness management has finally recognised it.

What are you going to do about it?' And once staff are confident that they are being told the truth, and that management and staff are in it together, you have taken the first step in the rebuilding process.

## 2. SET UP PERMANENT AND COMPREHENSIVE METHODS OF COMMUNICATION

The next step is to establish permanent, regular, predictable and comprehensive methods of communication based on the same principles:

- Make these methods a major underpinning component of the culture you are seeking to develop: a culture of frankness, dialogue, progress and reasoned optimism.

- We live in an era when the fastest, most effective, most accessible methods of communication are changing and improving almost daily. Try to use them all. Flash emails and notes round when something big happens, so that staff know immediately. If it works for you, use Twitter, Facebook and other social media. Put up display boards and update them frequently.

- Ask for invitations to any significant internal meetings: always accept the ones you get – go and speak.

- If you aren't invited to a meeting which you feel it is important you should go to, ask why and turn up anyway. People will probably be not just surprised but delighted and start to ask you to come along regularly.

- Open up a real dialogue with them. Show them what you and they face and that a path forward is being constructed. But also weigh up how effectively the meeting is working and what new arrangements may be needed.

- Don't forget about new staff. They will remember that you took the time to go and talk to them at a time (perhaps at induction) when they will be at sea and have very little understanding of their new workplace. But they do read the papers and are likely to have friends who have heard about the problems or are members of staff.

- It's really important you give them a full and credible picture, warts and all. As well as being a captive audience, they're also a very diverse and large one (with normal turnover), so the message will quickly infuse every corner of the organisation.

## 3. ASSURE PEOPLE THAT YOU ARE NOT SIMPLY REPORTING ON A DYING BUSINESS

- You need to say what you have found and what is being done to resuscitate the organisation or business.

- You need increasingly to be conveying an approach that works – in short, real results are needed.

- What you say has to stand up.

- Your analysis and predictions, some of which may be glaringly obvious but some of which won't be, also have to prove robust.

This might sound a Herculean task but it's simply about doing your best consistently. If you are telling it how it is, you are inevitably telling people how and who you are. And people will make a reasonable judgement in those circumstances. They don't expect perfection and they don't expect a flawless performance. They wouldn't believe it either. You become credible because you're imperfect, but you are achieving results.

## 4. INVITE AND WELCOME TESTING AND CHALLENGING OF YOUR IDEAS

- You will have gone a long way in communicating with people and sharing your ideas with them. But the fact that they are engaged does not mean they will be totally and permanently convinced.

- You have to show that you are open and listening, and that you mean what you say.

- Testing yourself fully and rigorously, letting others push you and influence you while maintaining and developing a consistent line, will all be part of building credibility. With that the recovery can really take off.

A symbolic debate – look at it as a test or as a confrontation – may well be necessary to achieve a symbolic compact. It will be worth it if you listen, hold your ground and show that you will act. In one organisation I went into, I needed to change the view of a leading doctor who had been misled about the real commitment of the previous regime to solving rather than masking the problem he faced. He made his concerns and suspicions very clear to me in a pivotal meeting with 20 staff who were crucial to delivery of this objective. I went through his concerns point by point, explaining how it would be different this time and making a public commitment that I would have to fulfil. After a silence that seemed like an eternity but was probably a few seconds, he warily agreed we should try again – but properly this time. I was as good as my word, and he as his: he was actually a brilliant but frustrated implementer. We made enormous strides very quickly as a result: we moved from 30% to 80% of patients being seen promptly in our Emergency Department.

An account of such debates will very definitely go round, particularly among key staff because it will have been a key debate. And there will be a clear message: things are going to change, it's worth getting on board.

# Reaching outside

As failure deepens and becomes evident internally, problems, especially if they are organisation-wide, will probably go public. Negative media attention will then typically create a crisis of its own, which will then have to be dealt with. This has happened widely in the banking industry with more and more questions raised about the culture and ethics of modern banking – about an 'anything you can get away with' approach from individuals, allegedly allowed or ignored by those in charge, be it to manipulate basic lending rates via LIBOR setting or to launder money from Iran or drug cartels.

In a completely different field, a firestorm has ravaged G4S's reputation because of its abject failure to provide necessary security for the

London Olympics and the stories that then emerged of its failures elsewhere. This was despite the fact that it was and is a highly profitable company with a worldwide reach. The Olympics security fiasco cost it a mere $80 million but the reputational effect was to wipe $1 billion off its share price.

If such hostile, adverse reporting is not dealt with, it will inevitably keep the organisation in the failure phase. It will demoralise and sap what little confidence there is outside and start to discredit new management. If not dealt with, it will become a prime example of the 'dead cat bounce' (see page 34).

So what should you be looking out for?

- There is always a time delay between what is actually happening and what is reported to the outside world. When bad news breaks, it will describe what has already happened. It may be relatively recent but it could be well in the past.

- Even worse, once the bad reputation is established, there is a smear by association: 'This new bit of bad news should not come as a surprise in an organisation that has already got all these other things wrong.'

- But because there is a lag you are likely to be remedying what is wrong.

- So the next step is to go out and tell the world the truth: the full bad news, and the good news they haven't yet heard about. Carefully highlighting this will help you to turn the story round.

- The connections that are made are often spurious. With careful handling, separate issues can be shown to be separate.

Underlying all this is the key point in the Yosemite curve where perception and reality separate. You must bring perception and reality together in dealing with the negative publicity and responding to it. If you try to manage perception and reality apart, you will confuse yourself and others and destroy your credibility. But most importantly, don't get too caught up. Remain calm, respond carefully, meet deadlines, avoid any form of self-imposed rushing. In those two famous words: 'DON'T PANIC'!

# Responding

So how should an organisation respond? Not by doing nothing. Not by saying nothing. Not by waiting passively and having responses dragged out of it. This is what needs to be done …

## 1. YOU MUST BE VISIBLE

React, comment, whatever. However hard it is, however difficult the story, it is better to be seen to be responding – even saying that you don't know, but you are looking into the matter. Sometimes, for a short while, you may be unsure what to do or unable to say what you are doing, but these should be rare exceptions because they will cost you dearly. They will tell the media and the public that the story must be right, that you are so nonplussed you are unable to say anything. This is almost never the case.

## 2. YOU MUST BE OPEN – AND SHOW THAT YOU ARE

- Respond to any allegations made as fully as you can.

- Acknowledge publicly what people already know is wrong.

- There will be other things wrong that they don't know about. Get these out in the open right away.

- Try not to give the appearance that things are being dragged out of you unwillingly and you are only commenting when you have no choice.

- Try to give more of the picture; show that things are more complex and many-sided. This will divert people from simplistic accounts or judgements. It will show the dilemmas and the many shades of grey in your story.

- Take things forward beyond what you have to concede so that a fuller, more positive picture is presented.

- Publicly set yourself some simple targets for matters you can see are already on the way to being put right. Chosen carefully, the early success that you will be able to report will help to show the public that real progress is being made.

## 3. GET OFF THE BACK FOOT

- Tell your story from the outset. If you have no story, you will be merely commenting on the media's.

- Give your account of what is happening so that it makes sense and offers a view of the future. That way, you have a chance of making your account the story.

- Persist at it. In Bath, as we were beginning the turnaround, we had to create a vision of what we would do …

### Creating a vision at the Royal United Hospital, Bath

Not long after the star ratings report, the Editor of the *Bath Chronicle* asked me to talk at a 'Bath Business Breakfast' – a monthly event for 80 senior figures from around Bath. My strategy was simple. I set out what had gone wrong, fully and frankly. I then showed all the progress we were already making to put right what was fundamentally wrong. I set out our ambition to do things far better than the average NHS hospital because the potential for the Royal United Hospital was so great and the dedication and commitment of its staff meant that we could achieve so much.

As I talked, I could feel the audience realising what had happened, empathising with our dilemma, understanding what we were trying to do, and willing us on. At the end I got a rousing round of applause.

As people were starting to leave, the Editor came up to me and said: 'Jan, that was fantastic. I'd like to put something about this in the paper right away. Can I get a health reporter to come and interview you?' I agreed before he could change his mind and spent some time helping the health reporter to turn my slides into a two-page spread headed 'Why our hospital will become the envy of the NHS' – the same subject as my talk.

# Retaining momentum

Once the immediate crisis is over and the media, the public and customers start to believe that the business or organisation recognises what has gone wrong, and is not leaving everything to fester, they will begin to listen to the warts-and-all version of events, including its positive side. They will still be suspicious, of course, but they will give those doing the confessing a chance.

- Change gear and build up your own stories. People all too often see crisis in isolation and breathe a sigh of relief when it is over.

- Keep up the good news and be visible.

- Once you have established your story, you must keep on describing it and showing it is true. Opportunities will present themselves, positive things will happen, targets will be achieved.

- Take these achievements to the media, in easy pre-digested form. There is every reason to expect them to take them on board and publish them.

- Move on from individual illustrations of your story to accounts of your organisation as one which is thriving in every respect.

- At some point you may even get unduly good publicity. Don't worry about this. On a scale of 1 (minor) to 10 (very bad), a press story which says that you are worse than you are is generally 8, 9 or 10. One that says you are better than you really are is usually 1 or 2.

# Trumpeting success

As soon as you get any success, trumpet it. Create an expectation of achievement and celebration. It offers a tremendous springboard to go further and show that the organisation has realistic plans to go beyond the average and become exceptional. The attention that has had to be given to building up the reputation to date will have created fertile ground and there will be enough things going on, enough energy in the organisation, to provide the stories to support this. At about this time, the realisation that you are now getting much better will hit everyone. Then you will finally be out of the woods.

## Implementing primary targeting of lists at Medway Hospital

The NHS Regional Director was going through our Performance Improvement Plan with us. Before we could begin our presentation, he informed us that a new way of sifting and ordering waiting lists to enable them to be better managed had been developed. The new system was called primary targeting of lists (PTL). Everyone needed to take on board the lessons and adopt them, particularly hospitals like us. We confessed that we had not heard of this wonderful new system. As he was going through our figures, he noted that the trend in our inpatient and outpatient waiting lists was consistently and steeply downwards, well beyond the national trend.

We explained how we had analysed the make-up of our waiting lists and the way in which patients were being booked on to them differently by different secretaries and clerks on different instructions from each consultant, with chaotic or random results. Many patients were seen or operated on after fairly short waits. Others were randomly selected for operation at any time. Because so many slots had been filled as a result of the first two actions, lots of patients waited the maximum allowable time, before there was a huge scramble to get them operated on quickly.

We told him how we had realised this was a self-created problem. We drew simple graphs of what was happening and then created simple graphs of what a well-managed waiting list should look like. We worked through the changes in booking behaviour that would be necessary to create it, and saw how simple these were. We then began a simple education process in reforming booking, and gradually standardised procedures to make it easier.

Finally, we explained how, with a much more accurate assessment of the capacity we needed and what we had, we were able to plan to do the right amount of work and achieve reductions.

▶

The Regional Director was startled at first: 'Your waiting lists are reducing, whereas everywhere else they are going up.' Then the penny dropped. 'You have implemented PTL, and not even those who invented it have done that. We are going to have to get you to explain to others how to do this.' Within days, key staff at our hospital were being invited to lecture regionally and nationally on how to implement PTL. At one fell swoop we had moved from dunces to pioneers.

## To sum up ...

In a deeply failing organisation, communication will have clogged up. It will not be doing its proper job. Getting it going is the *sine qua non* of beginning to get everything else right.

And the place to start is with your team, with your people, but moving quickly on to those who are absolutely key to your success but outside: customers, funders, your public or audience, regulators, etc. Thinking through what you have to say, what you are trying to and need to get across, and how, is vital – as is how you listen and respond. And it's just as vital to get this cascading through the organisation: not just one person, but a team; not just a team, but everyone. And it's progressive: you can get off the back foot, build your credibility and reputation, and consolidate each gain you make. Finally, trumpet your success, use communication to make it infectious.

So, as the key issue of improving communication is tackled, what else needs to be done? Cue the next chapter.

# 8

# Getting back in control

In Chapter 7 I described how to get people's attention, re-engage them, win support and start to build momentum to put things right. This is the necessary first step. But much more has to follow. Real control has to be regained. Workable solutions have to be found. They have to be implemented. In this chapter I will show how all this is done.

## Digging till you find the cause

Explanations of what is failing and why will be rife. These might be good as far as they go, but will probably be incomplete. Work needs to start right away on the problems that everyone has agreed on, in order to show some quick progress. But, as a matter of the utmost

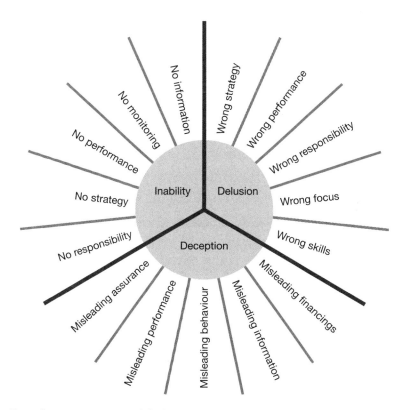

*Finding the root cause of failure*

priority, the root cause must be found. Look for three simple things: inability, delusion and deception. These will lead to the root cause.

Here are some ideas for how to find *your* root cause:

- Listen, absorb, reflect.
- Reach out and talk to as many people as possible, to understand their perceptions, assumptions and expectations – many of which will be mutually conflicting.
- Put these together and reconcile them. This will give you a real sense of the prevailing culture.
- Ensure you have a yardstick of what the culture should be.
- Measure and judge the culture you have found against your yardstick.

It is only when you have done this that you will be able to find the solutions that are needed. The problems you unearth are likely to be fundamental, but you will also discover that problems which others have identified are not really problems: something else is going on.

- Keep digging until you find the root cause, because otherwise you will bury it and all your efforts will be as useful as putting sticking plaster on a bleeding wound.
- Use symptoms (notably the six warning signals described in detail in Chapters 4 and 5) to give you clues as to where to look for the root cause.
- As soon as you have identified the root cause, bring it out. You will be challenging conventional wisdom on the reasons for failure and you need to do it determinedly.
- Remember, as a newcomer, you have important temporary advantages that it is vital to use. If you don't, you can quickly become part of the problem.
- Act quickly, even though bringing things out increases the perception (not the reality) of failure.
- Your analysis must lead not only to short-term action but also to the unfolding of a broad strategy, so that your staff and

your bosses (i.e. whoever you are accountable to) can see that there is a clear and coherent way forward to reduce and ultimately solve the organisation's problems. Setting out the broad strategy takes time but it must be done at the outset and continued into the future.

Once you have found the root cause, it becomes possible – even relatively straightforward – to find strategies to remove it. The root problem may be unknowingly determining behaviours or strategies, so that people do not realise they are being led astray. When I started to get to know Medway, for example, I realised that many of the behaviours that seemed to me odd or wrong derived from the perceived need to get a new hospital at virtually any cost. It was then relatively straightforward to change them to meet our real needs.

Having discovered what the wrong driver for the organisation has been and stopped it, it is important to identify what the real drivers should be. If one hasn't got a prior view, this shouldn't be too difficult. The key is to ask:

- What are the measures of the organisation's success as seen by others (customers, investors, regulators)?

- What was it that made those others deem the organisation to be failing?

# Tackling immediate problems

One other thing needs to be done immediately. Without doubt, there will be large, immediate problems rearing up in your face. You are in the middle of failure and no one has been tackling the problems successfully for some while. The key point is that the problems are explicitly identified and action is taken on them immediately. The problems might relate to finance, immediate operational difficulties, insufficient capacity/volume/output, lack of information and, related to that, lack of organisational grip. Operational problems are the most obvious, the most various and the most frequent. Here's an example about car parking, about as generic and common an operational issue as you could wish for.

# Dealing with gridlock at Medway

When I got the job of CEO at Medway, the two key things that you could not help seeing were that it had an almost completely new hospital building and that everyone was unhappy. How could this be? Enlightenment came when I noticed that outside the hospital there was semi-permanent gridlock. There were queues all day on all the key roads within the hospital as people tried to get through, to park or to get out. This meant that, not infrequently, ambulances trying to get to A&E were caught in a queue of cars. Local residents were irritated as they had a permanent jam just outside the hospital grounds and people were trying to park in the street to avoid the queues. To cap it all, there were insufficient spaces, so patients and staff were often unable to park. So absolutely everyone was irritated on a daily basis by this dysfunction.

The flow pattern of cars simply made no sense. Instead of having a flow of vehicles from the entrance past the main departments to A&E, we decided to map out another route, so that all patient and visitor cars stayed on the road around the periphery (which we made one-way), and we created a separate entry and exit for the car park. They got to and from the parking area without going near the main entrances, leaving the central road free and restricting it to vehicles which genuinely needed to go that way. In a trice, the queues evaporated. Local residents saw major improvements in their streets. The newspapers and the council, which had been pillorying the hospital for the mess, actually noticed and were pleased.

This left the problem of the lack of car parking. An ill-fated scheme to build a multi-storey car park to coincide with the opening of the hospital had collapsed a few months before and there were no other plans in place. I was told that the council was now 'green' and would not entertain proposals for extra car parking to meet our needs. 'Don't even bother asking for anything, they will humiliate you!'

I decided to meet the supposed arch-enemy of hospital car parking, the Director of Planning and Transportation. After about

10 minutes talking round the subject, it slowly dawned on us that we were each labouring under the misconception that our opinions differed. In fact our views on the extra car parking the hospital needed and how it might be provided were identical. The council had not been opposed to sensible plans, but was simply fed up of what it saw as a 'fiddling while Rome burns' attitude and wanted a sensible but not dogmatic recognition of environmental concerns.

We agreed what needed to be done. Within two months we put forward a plan and it was approved. With the council's help the hospital's car parking problems were solved.

The people who have stuck it out as things have gone badly wrong will almost certainly already have done a great deal under intense pressure but they will be struggling. What they need is a sense that they are making progress, including recognising what they have already achieved. Where recovery is not recognised or is seen as remission, the best way to accelerate it is to create a mindset based on open-mindedness and trust. It should involve early recognition and reinforcement of success, driving everyone into a virtuous circle of improvement.

With the right understanding and support, people's actions become less desperate, less stressed and more balanced. If they have the confidence that they will be supported through their reasonable difficulties and mistakes, and that their improvements will be recognised, they sleep more easily and perform better. Here are some guidelines:

- Pinpoint the problem, open it up for scrutiny and obtain full information (typically numerical).

- Divide the problem into easy, doable bits and harder ones that will initially resist your efforts. The old adage about how to eat an elephant – in bite-size bits – applies. So, as soon as you can, do those 'easy, doable bits'!

- Explain how you are doing it: use a clear methodology and set short-term targets that you know you will reach if you are systematic and careful. I did this at the Royal United Hospital, Bath. Each time we reached a target – and I set easy ones first – we celebrated it and told anyone who would listen about our success. The result was that the staff involved became much more self-confident and motivated, and knew they were and would be supported.

- Recognise the specific improvement rather than measuring against an absolute standard.

- Then, using that confidence and motivation, get onto the more difficult issues. The staff whom you need to deliver realise that the once seemingly impossible is now distinctly doable, and are actually quite keen to do it!

Tackling an obviously hard problem can also have tremendous symbolic significance. This is often exemplified in a very powerful but resistant or entrenched group. It was clear only weeks after I started a new job that such a group (in this case, of surgeons) had to be challenged head on – or disaster would follow, because their practices suited them but at the expense of the organisation's smooth running. I met the group and told them that practices would have to change to avert the impending disaster. They pointed out that this would have an adverse effect upon their service, which was already teetering on the brink. Despite this, I insisted, believing that temporising would make an unacceptable position worse and could lead to a collapse in the service. This is (metaphorically) what I said: 'I am opening a door here that we must all walk through. Now we have all walked through it I am closing it. Here is the key. I am locking the door and, look, I am throwing away the key.' I made it clear that there was no going back – a fairly risky strategy for a new unknown, but one I felt I had to adopt. The results came swiftly: the risk of disaster disappeared, I kept being stopped in the corridor, an unknown of three weeks' standing, by one senior figure after another, who congratulated me on finally doing something about what they saw as a festering problem – and what's more, the service itself improved.

Here's another example with central importance for the business concerned.

## St Albans elective care centre

West Hertfordshire Hospitals NHS Trust opened a new elective care centre in St Albans in September 2007. It was part of a sound plan to rationalise and separate emergency and planned services. It opened a month before the Trust was precipitated into deep failure by being, for the second year running, joint worst in the country, in the annual hospital star ratings, with the subsequent resignation of its Chief Executive. On my arrival in November as the new Chief Executive, it was explained to me that the elective care centre was part of the solution not the problem, but it had 'teething problems'. Together with my equally new Chief Operating Officer we had a look at what was going on. Two weeks in, we met and shared our conclusions: it didn't have 'teething problems'; it was an implementation disaster.

Why was this? It was overspending at a catastrophic rate and at the same time was completely unable to deal with the numbers of patients it had planned and needed to treat, thereby putting a huge amount of pressure on patient waits. When we looked into it, we saw what had happened. An implementation process had been set in train but it had not been monitored or followed through rigorously, and managers had not been held to account for identifying and correcting problems, so they built up and multiplied.

The first problem was that it had been assumed that staff would transfer from their existing hospital to St Albans, where the work was moving. Many chose not to do this. The Trust had a rigid recruitment freeze. Those planning the elective care centre felt they couldn't recruit to replace the staff who didn't transfer. This created staffing gaps. One response was to try to run operating theatres with fewer staff, but this proved impossible, so operating theatres were in many cases partially staffed but unable to run, with the result that patients weren't treated but major staffing costs were still incurred. As this began to be realised managers did everything they could to run the operating theatres, buying in temporary agency staff to do so. However, the agency staff were much more expensive than permanent staff, so running these sessions was extremely expensive. Because a number of sessions were being cancelled due to staff shortages, the hospital Trust was contractually required to ensure patients who had been cancelled (and there were many) were treated within a month of their cancellation date. Obviously lacking the capacity to do this themselves, they had to send patients to private hospitals at a premium rate.

So each of the tactics cost a great deal of money, creating an absolutely enormous overspend. But the root cause was clear: there was no proper culture of performance management with clear accountability for following through and achieving organisational goals. We changed this and in changing it ensured there was realism about which theatre sessions we could staff. Those we couldn't realistically staff, we closed down and saved the money on. We began and built up a vigorous recruitment effort and gradually reduced our use of temporary staff. Quickly we reduced most of the overspend and within a few months we eliminated it. The capacity of the theatres was increased as we increased staffing, leading to fewer cancellations and virtually eliminating the costly need to outsource work. The original plan had been sound but there was a fundamental failure of implementation and follow-through.

# Rebuilding the mechanisms for managing

The next things that will need to be looked at are the structure, the team and the processes of the organisation. The mechanisms for managing will have fallen into partial or total disuse. Mechanisms having any usefulness should be resurrected, but the existing framework has failed and will need amendment and probably radical alteration. There will be little time to assess and act but the shortage of time can bring advantages:

- Plump for simple, inclusive, action-oriented mechanisms which everyone will be able to see are working.

- Be transparent: people should be able to see how their work relates to other work and who is responsible for what.

- Two-way communication must permeate the arrangements.

- Avoid as far as you can organising around the classic function-based silos of responsibility: operations, finance, HR, etc. By all means use these, but make them supportive.

- Articulate your structure around what people do, and the processes that define their work.

- Do not atomise or balkanise. Make connections critical to your structure.

- Above all, test that what is being created is an approach that is competent enough to tackle massive problems.

- Make sure the structure is able to get the many capable and key people on board who will be looking for a signal that they are wanted.

- Make accountability and responsibility absolutely clear – with clear consequences if either fails. People should not be able to say they have done their bit, but nothing seems to happen, they don't know how to make it happen, or it isn't for them to do so.

- Agree objectives, monitor performance and manage performance.

- Then devolve, devolve, devolve, but monitor explicitly and be seen to do so, on occasion by attending and actively participating in devolved meetings.

- Show that this level of oversight is also about support and enablement, so that people know that they are able to act.

Instead of simply ticking over, you can now really crank up the engine to drive forward. You should by now have put together a confident, determined, outgoing team who are committed to solving problems and who will be buttressed by your belief in them and their belief in themselves.

The overwhelming majority of your staff will be capable but in need of reassurance, support and possibly redirection. It is therefore crucial to signal your own positive judgements clearly and quickly. Don't leave the Sword of Damocles hanging over people. Tell them they have your confidence, and why. It will send a wave of relief and motivation through the organisation. People will think: 'Not only is there a way forward – which looks as though it will work – but I am part of it!'

A very small number of people, unfortunately, are usually part of the problem. They have mismanaged or misdefined the problem and don't have the skills to work differently. If they can't be placed somewhere else useful, it is vital to agree their exit quickly. They should be able to leave with dignity both for their sakes and for the message it gives to those who remain. Avoid any 'night of the long knives'. Make the message considered and the transition considerate.

# Unlocking the organisation

The next step is to build and deliver across the organisation. Much of this is about reshaping and restructuring, changing the organisation's culture and raising morale. As described earlier in this book, a failing organisation typically suffers from fragmentation, passivity and fatalism; everyday processes have ceased to work or are only functioning on autopilot. The key to opening such a 'locked' organisation is getting the people within it to believe that a driving force exists to which they can respond, and in so doing can take part in renewing it. Demoralised staff, once they are convinced that they have a part to play in the future, become the solution rather than the problem.

Systems and processes need to function smoothly and in line with an organisation's needs. When the organisation fails they cease to do this, they fall apart. Look (on the next page) at the failure trajectory with processes in mind.

So how do you build or rekindle processes? Personal commitment from leadership is essential. This involves understanding what is required and having the determination to carry it through. Where those who identify barriers don't have the power to remove them, assistance must be given, even extra resources. If this approach is

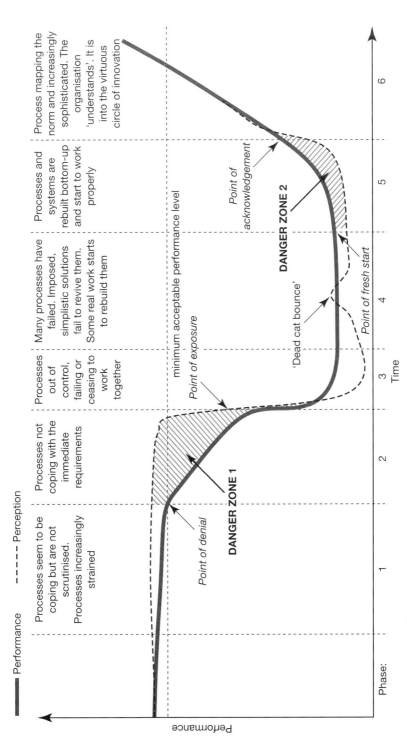

*The process story of failing organisations*

adopted, it becomes self-sustaining and spreads across the organisation with decreasing resistance and increasing enthusiasm as positive results are seen.

The key initial steps I have described above are the prerequisites to getting into recovery. To embed and consolidate recovery requires the organisation to start firing on all cylinders. This means starting to work organically, cohesively and purposefully. Bear in mind:

- The recovery phase from failure typically raises staff morale and makes staff believe in themselves. This in turn can unleash huge enthusiasm and determination to do things better – a huge potential to innovate.

- If carefully utilised, this can catapult the recovering organisation into a leading organisation.

- Because it is disruptive, deep and radical innovation is less likely in smoothly functioning, untroubled organisations. But the conditions can be just right as you come out of the disruption of failure into the uplands of recovery.

## Process redesign at Medway

At Medway Hospital when we started to implement a redesign of basic processes, it became evident that this was creating big improvements around the organisation and, very importantly, it was based on the insights of existing staff. As a result, individuals and teams offered to redesign other processes that they thought were defective. They felt confident that they would be supported by management, and they were. There was a blossoming of constructive process redesign, with the result that everything started to be done better throughout the organisation. An organisation that I had been told on my arrival was 'universally mediocre' was in less than three years lauded as 'bristling with innovation' by none other than the Secretary of State for Health.

It is vital that you don't stop once you have achieved 'average'. Go for exceptional and you will achieve it. The satisfaction, when it is publicly acknowledged that the organisation is flying, is immense and an enormous morale booster. A great and indisputable example of this comes from a now universally known and respected firm, Toyota. Toyota rose from being an impoverished, patronised assembler of cars in the wake of Japan's total defeat in the Second World War to become the world's most successful manufacturing company. It started getting it right in the 1950s and 1960s. It has continued to do so ever since (notwithstanding a few well-publicised problems with safety recalls). That's what we all need to do.

## To sum up ...

Finding the root cause of the failure, which is often partly obvious but usually partly concealed, is critical to moving forward. Once it is found, there is firm ground to move forward on. And the first thing to do is to get stuck in to immediate, graspable problems, even if they appear minor or incidental; show progress on them, give the business some life. From there, a more permanent, structured approach can be used, rebuilding structures and processes so they are explicitly and freshly fit for purpose. With those in place, systematic delivery becomes feasible. Managers need to be able to do things. This sequence is designed to enable them to.

In the next part of the book, I will discuss the attributes and skills that 'doing' managers need.

# part four

# Succeeding

*It is better to be roughly right than precisely wrong.*
JOHN MAYNARD KEYNES

The genesis of this book was experiencing failure and learning from it, a compelling enough theme on its own, particularly as it is such a neglected one. It is important. We can understand a great deal from it. But if that's all then what I have written and observed would be an account, hopefully a persuasive and graphic account, of *what not to do*, what to avoid, negative management commandments.

But I realised that you can't really say what not to do without having a strong and sound implicit idea of *what to do*. Avoiding failure and getting out of it require positive management behaviours. I have described many of these in previous chapters. They are the essence of good management, the opposite of failure. In the remainder of this book I put these positives together and propose a different management approach. I argue that good managers are catalysts, pathway finders and releasers of potential.

In setting out my stall, I will help readers gauge what difference my approach can make to what they can achieve and also what it cannot do, because knowing the limits of your own approach is the key to success. My approach really does help managers not just to have success but to be enduringly successful.

And it really can be embedded so that it survives changes of personnel. In some cases, it has survived people changing around me, and in other cases, it has survived my own departure. It works and it lasts. And its principles are relevant to everyone. It is not specifically aimed at those who wish to scale the towering heights of management, though they probably won't scale them unless they do understand it. It is about how organisations work, and understanding that will make *any* manager a better manager. It is management for every man and every woman.

# 9

# The opposite of failure

Before I can credibly describe managerial approaches which work, will succeed and should produce the intended results, it is essential that I lay the positive foundation stones that will enable these things to happen. They are the opposites to many of the things I have described so far and they make sense in their own right. I will set them out in this chapter and build on them in the rest of the book.

## Five key ideas

There are five key ideas which underpin my notion of what management is about, what we should recognise and what we should strive for as managers.

### IDEA 1: DON'T BE TOO CONCERNED WITH THE OUTSTANDING

- Survival is about being sufficiently good.
- This does not mean a lack of ambition or a messy compromise.
- It is realistic; it is hard.
- It means knowing how you are measured and how that changes.
- It is achievable.
- It is permanent.

Imperfection characterises our world. Our understanding and our achievement are always imperfect. That means we will always need to do better. But the obverse of this is that if you are imperfect you *can* do better; there is something to aim for. If we keep seeking what are in effect extreme behaviours, at an extreme end of the spectrum, we will fail to learn how to behave in more normal, typical circumstances and we won't have the sense of what we should give to our organisation and what our organisation should give to us.

Healthy people are not super athletes. Super athletes punish their bodies and become atypical specimens, brilliantly adapted for an extraordinarily special task and, by definition, not a model for others. They are about competition until only one is left.

It's not just about our bodies either. The psychotherapist D.W. Winnicott gave us the concept of the 'good-enough mother' – the 'ordinary devoted mother ... an example of the way in which the foundations of health are laid down by the ordinary mother in her ordinary loving care of her own baby'. Don't dismiss the imperfect and the ordinary. Understand them, appreciate them.

## IDEA 2: DON'T SEE SUCCESS AS AN END POINT

- Good business is about continuing and continuous delivery.
- Real success is about: resilience, sustaining delivery, meeting new challenges, and staying in the game and on the ball.

This idea is so fundamental to what I have to say that I have been trailing it right from the beginning (see page xxiv). To repeat, avoid the trap of seeing failure as a state, and success as something that is impressive and laudable but passes quickly. Realise that it depends on you whether failure and success are states or points you pass through. You must take action to make failure a point you come out of. You must also take action to keep in a long-term state of success. The opposite state to failure is not short-term success but rather sustained achievement, success-FUL-ness.

With Idea 2 I am also seeking to put right another commonplace error in the received view of management. Repetition, constancy, survival and continuation may all be boring, but they are essential. We need to learn, relearn and remaster them. Exceptional success is fleeting and often unreal, and does not tell us what to do between the fleeting moments. So my message is:

- Keep going.
- Realise that there will always be new problems, new challenges and new errors.
- Be ready for them; look for them.

- Never see an end point or a particular target as a be-all and end-all.
- Targets are markers on the route you must continue on.
- Miss them and you have probably taken a wrong turning.
- Hit one and you still have to move forward.

## IDEA 3: PERFECTION IN MANAGEMENT IS AN ILLUSION

- Real managers – good managers – are imperfect managers.
- They get things wrong, they realise that, and they learn from their mistakes.
- Good managers support managers who make mistakes.
- They take responsibility alongside them.
- They forgive them, so enabling learning and improvement.

Perfection tends to mean that an ideal and absolutely right end point can be reached. Imperfection, on the other hand, is about the messy everyday business of not fully understanding a problem, not necessarily getting it exactly right first time, but trying again until one does get it right, never giving up. It's about being balanced and unfazed by what doesn't conform to the perfection trajectory, ready to go on and do something different, to learn some new tricks.

### Hospital error rates

Recognising imperfection means looking for and acknowledging errors. Drug errors in hospitals were for many years rated at 3 in every 1000 cases or 0.3%. With computerisation of drug prescribing, an early adopter hospital (a famous US hospital) used a computer to check individual drug prescriptions against the required protocols. The computer detected an error rate of over 3%, but these errors were different from the ones forming the 0.3%. The hospital decided to get to the bottom of this and put

▶

a team in various areas of the hospital for a month, painstakingly checking every prescription in tedious detail. They found an error rate of 5%, but the errors they found were largely different ones, making a total error rate of over 8%. The hospital now knew what mistakes were being made and did something about it. Other hospitals undoubtedly had similar error rates in practice, but carried on happily thinking theirs was 0.3%.

Which hospital would you prefer to be treated in?

It is not about slackness. It's about being able to carry on efficiently and effectively when things aren't perfect. It's about adaptability and flexibility, and not being ground to a standstill because something didn't quite work out or wasn't expected, but taking that in one's stride and moving forward along the right path.

The other positive side to recognising imperfection is that you are actually freed to do something before you are certain it is perfectly right. Good managers do things. Imperfect managers can do things. I received an email from a non-executive director who said, 'The results reported at the board today are a clear demonstration that good things do not just happen – they are made to happen.' What I have seen in failing organisations is an absence of the 'making'.

## 'Happening' and 'doing'

This contrast between 'things happening' and 'management doing' is illustrated repeatedly in revelations about insecure or lost data in many major organisations. For instance, an investigation by a senior city accountant into the loss of 25 million child benefit records, including bank details and sensitive personal information, by HM Revenue & Customs found 'no visible management of data security at any level' and officials demonstrating a 'muddle-through ethos'.

What I noticed at Medway was that checks and balances, standards and competencies were being taken for granted. If something went wrong in a process, the error was reported, but the system that was supposed to pick up that error and then ensure its cause was found and corrected was no longer working properly; most importantly, there was no one there to monitor that it was no longer working properly. Mistakes weren't being corrected and used to learn better behaviour. One minor failure had led to another, and another, and so performance had started to spiral downwards.

Once the behaviour of staff involved in these processes was understood and coordinated, something could be done about the problem. Those same staff had the necessary skills and could work out the answers; they just needed to be supported and given the right context. When action replaces muddle-through, you are on the road to solving your problems. As *doers*, managers can maximise their organisation's achievements.

## IDEA 4: EVOLVE AND ADAPT

- Living organisms evolve and adapt.
- They are sensitive to their ever changing environment.
- So are imperfect managers.
- They scrutinise the ground beneath their feet and the distant horizon – and everything in between.
- 'Imperfect management' provides the conditions for businesses and other organisations to live and do things better.
- It makes them thrive, hang together.
- It means they build up a resistance to all the things that create failure, and an ability to shake them off.

This idea is separate but it is also a completer. Self-correction, rebalancing, coping and fault tolerance are all possible and are all enhanced if you don't unnecessarily make things worse. The virtue of a course of action needs to be balanced against its adverse consequences. Many managerial ideas only focus on their benefits. This can create a blinkered short-termism. The success happens, but who is around to account for the failure? This is true of the goals and ends of businesses but it is also true of what happens within them.

## IDEA 5: AVOID BIG SHIFTS

- Avoid making quantum leaps for their own sake.

- They create risk and can destroy sound organic functioning – sometimes for ever.

- 'If it ain't broke, don't fix it.'

- Show some humility.

- See innovation as growth, building, *not* creative destruction.

- 'Above all, do no harm' – attributed to Hippocrates, father of medicine, and beloved of arguably the first real hospital manager, Florence Nightingale.

At the micro level, if you permit violence to be done to the values of a business, you start to degrade it, to make it lose its vitality and healthiness. This has dreadful consequences in the long term. If, for example, you sacrifice honesty and straightforwardness to achieve your ends, the business will cease to value these qualities and will forget about them, and it will suffer. If you see innovation as an unqualified good, something we have to do even though we don't know what it is, and the status quo as dispensable, you may inadvertently, carelessly, destroy crucial aspects of the workings of your business. An insider in a once famous and FTSE top 100 electronics and IT company told me, 'We innovated like crazy, and we went out of business.'

If you cut corners on safety or competence to achieve more, more quickly, then the lesser valuation of safety and competence will come back and hit you. You will have achieved something, but you will have done harm. To preserve the vitality of a business, its ability to come back to a happy resting point, its homeostasis, there needs to be a powerful bias towards these last two principles. It's a bit like the centre of gravity: stray too far from it and you will fall over. If it is strong, it will pull you back to the right place.

# Adapting

The fundamental difference between soundly functioning businesses and failing ones is coherence and unity on the one hand and fragmentation and insular behaviour on the other. So why one or the other? Is there a pattern? What is the glue that enables coherence?

The pattern I have found is of positive and negative change through time:

- *either* a failure to change and adapt to meet changing circumstances, often accompanied by a failure to recognise the need to adapt;

- *or* a more positive process of adapting, evolving, growing, and eventually, hopefully after a long period of survival and doing well, fading away and maybe disappearing.

Organic life survives and evolves by adaptation. Adaptation is itself a response to a failure, in order to deal with new circumstances. A failure to adapt is ultimately a death sentence for a species. The mutant, the adaptor, the extra evolved organism is the one that doesn't fail or responds to the potential failure and moves on to success. And so it is with businesses, organisations and management.

Businesses or units within them can be quite small and apparently simple, possibly only a handful of people making and selling a single product. Even here, though, a business of any durability builds up experience, practice, competence and an ability to respond to the varied and unpredictable demands of everyday life. A business comes into being to meet a need, and if it does so successfully, then it thrives, flourishes and endures. It is a truism that businesses are at their most vulnerable when they are small, new to this world and, in varying degrees, naïve, innocent and inexperienced. If they don't learn and develop fast, they run into trouble and fail; in all probability they cease to exist.

Now apply this very simple idea to the much larger businesses that typify the workaday world and in which most of us spend our working time. Bigger, established businesses comprise hundreds or thousands of people and will have been around for a fair while. The variety of skills, experience and understanding within them will be enormous and most of it will be located in the individuals who work there. It will be interconnected, interrelated, interdependent, because each particular understanding, expertise and experience will need to be complemented and validated by others, to add all the value it can to enable good products to be produced, to enable development to take place and to enable the business to react and grow.

To have a long, healthy life one needs to avoid illness, deal with it when it occurs and do what it takes to remain fit and healthy. This is management's task in relation to the body of the business, the business organism. We need to know whether our business or our unit within it is healthy or not, what we need to do to make it healthy and thriving, how to recognise signs of ill health and how to do something about them before they become disabling and then fatal illnesses.

The business that achieved particular landmark success yesterday may be bankrupt today. Think of all the companies that have been swallowed up or disappeared. Look at:

- The shifting fortunes of computer companies, first impregnable IBM, then Apple, then Microsoft.

- The travails of Nokia, as its mobile phone market share and market leadership fell away at speed, heading towards Apple and Samsung.

- Kodak, the camera company, once synonymous with photographs and photography. It somehow missed out on the boom in digital photography despite helping to invent it, and declared itself bankrupt in January 2012.

- The ups and downs in the UK retail sector. Impregnable Marks & Spencer is down, then it's up, then down again; Sainsbury's similarly dips, and bobs up. Who would predict who's next?

Each of these businesses survived and thrived for a long while, and those that remain can and should still do so, but their managers must be striving not just for success but to sustain what they do successfully over a long period to have any chance of this. And this means recognising that the complexity of 'living' businesses is critical. It means:

- realising complexity exists;

- realising it will have a logic and an order even if it is seemingly incomprehensible;

- absolutely not treating it as mistaken and misguided – that will almost certainly lead to destruction and loss;

- preferably, though not always necessarily, understanding the organisation's logic;

- accessing it where possible;

- most importantly, utilising it and channelling it;

- in this way, creating health and development in the organisation;

- thereby solving the organisation's problems; and

- where it is failing, setting it firmly on the path to recovery.

Although this whole account has a deliberately positive and constructive tone, the managerial watchword is *vigilance*. Remember, many of this book's examples are from failing businesses. Growth and development based on deeply embedded understandings and processes can still get out of control and be destructive, just like the infections or cancerous growths within living bodies, and create failing businesses. Management needs to tap down to root behaviours, insights, experiences and skills, ensure they promote health, not dysfunction, and where organisational health has been lost, recover it.

# Giving and receiving feedback

Businesses and individual work units within them are (obviously) made up of real people with real emotions, feelings, behaviours and skills. What, then, provides the essential link, the binding together between the overall living organism and the real people who must make it work? It is communication. It is more than overhearing something, or the wind whistling past. When we communicate we convey what we know, we share it, we open it up for scrutiny, we allow others to modify and improve it and vice versa, we work as a whole rather than a part, we are understanding and we are cooperative. A business which works well, which communicates and in which people communicate, conveys information and processes it effectively.

## The importance of using feedback

When I took over West Hertfordshire Hospitals its staff assumed they were doing what patients wanted, but surveys showed that to be far from the case: we were creating much higher levels of dissatisfaction than other hospitals because we were not communicating with our patients, or with each other enough, or well enough. As a result many things were being done without proper thought and many expectations were being defeated. When I realised this, I got the organisation to look through exactly what we were failing on, and how we were failing to communicate, reassure patients and often meet their very basic needs. The reaction of staff was very instructive. It wasn't to say that none of this was true or that it was nothing to do with them. Instead they showed a huge determination to sort the problems out and proactively put in place systems to communicate with patients. Following directly from that response, a wide range of changes was brought in from the bottom up, using what staff knew and understood about patients. And at the heart of doing things better was consistent communication and taking responsibility for it. This is not just about uniting reality and perception. Here it means linking the perception and the reality to patients' expectations.

Good processing and good processes drive businesses. These processes have feedback loops: they are being changed constructively and positively all the time by the people in them, alert to what is going on around them and what is being communicated to them (see the diagram on the next page). When communications fail or cease to take place, processes that need feedback and responsiveness become stuck, default and cease to work effectively. They cease to respond to the changing world around them. They help precipitate failure.

Different bits of the body, different organs, undertake different processes, all of which combine to create the final effect. They do this

*The communication-feedback loop*

simultaneously – multi-tasking, if you like. Increasingly, we see computers being developed to do the same, though as yet in an infinitely simpler way. They receive information, compute it and place the results alongside other analytic and computational tasks that have been undertaken to result in a unified action. The functions of a nerve end, a cone in the eye, a tooth and a blood cell are utterly different but they combine to make the body work.

This process of cooperative differentiation is something to look for and applaud. It is not about demarcation. You only differentiate and do different things when it helps. But it is about skill and specialisation. And the more complex the task undertaken, the more one will be looking for effective cooperative differentiation and specialisation. Managed organisations can and should be understood and applauded in the same way.

## Differentiation in London

While writing this book I came across Peter Ackroyd's fascinating book, *London: The Biography*. One of the myriad insights in that book is that, as London grew and grew, it differentiated the skills of its citizens and made them much more particular than in smaller, simpler communities. This differentiation was part of what enabled London to grow and become more effective. This is how he puts it:

> *The segregation of districts within London, is also reflected in the curious fact that 'the London artisan rarely understands more than one department of the trade to which he serves his apprenticeship', while country workmen*

▶

*tend to know all aspects of their profession. It is another token of the 'specialisation' of London. By the 19th century the division and distinctions manifested themselves in the smallest place in the smallest trade ... 'the number of their branches and subdivisions is simply bewildering'; 'a man will go through life in comfort knowing but one infinitely small piece of work' ... So these workers became a small component of the intricate and gigantic mechanism which is London and London trade.*

Peter Ackroyd, *London: The Biography*
(Chatto & Windus, 2000), p. 126

Interestingly Ackroyd sees London on the one hand as a 'mechanism' but on the other as an organism; hence the expression 'the biography'. Of course, London and the businesses I talk about are both mechanisms and organisms.

# Managing relentlessly

The five ideas outlined at the beginning of this chapter can be used to pin down the 'evolution vector' which good, alert managers have, and with which they imbue their staff. Time and again in difficult situations, the managers who do well are not necessarily the cleverest people, and the management approaches that work are not the most sophisticated, but are those that keep going, come what may. The most robust technique is never to accept there is a brick wall, and to make each answer the springboard to solving the next question. It's about saying two things together. This is good enough for now. It will never be good enough for good.

When I started working to reduce waiting lists at Medway, my team and I were pioneers. There was no guidance available from anyone on what we had to do. So we tried one thing, and then another. If something half-worked, we developed it; we looked for new ideas from the new ground we had secured. But we always kept the ground we had secured. At first slowly, but then more rapidly, we made progress. When we looked back on what we had achieved, we could see the pathway we had trodden, but while we were doing it we had effectively been slashing through the undergrowth blindfolded. That is what I call relentless management. It's about trying things until they succeed and, as and when they do, building on them – endless iterations until a virtuous loop is created.

Relentless management isn't a form of megalomania, trying to and assuming you control everything. It's about:

- getting on top of a sufficient amount of what surrounds you to be able to act
- then acting
- reviewing that again, once you've reached some new, safer ground
- moving onto the next higher, safer bit of ground
- reducing the 20% error that had to be accepted today, by 80% tomorrow
- reducing the remaining 20% by 80% the day after that.

There will be a way through, even if it isn't the one that seemed likely initially, and even if it entails unpleasant consequences.

This shows other keys to relentlessness: pragmatism, opportunism, lateral thinking, and quite simply admitting error and starting again in a different direction. Relentless management ensures your work is based on a convincing narrative drive that fits the facts and the needs. You don't find out what story you are in, you choose to tell the story and help it unfold. So clear, well-thought-out, transparent systems and processes are essential aspects of thriving organisations.

- Relentless managers keep running. They know it's a marathon but that there are odd, sometimes unexpected sprints while it takes place.

My team had reduced the number of outpatients at risk of waiting more than the target of six months to a trickle. But there was still a risk that we would not be able to see them all by the deadline. They managed to track most down and persuade them to come in. Some couldn't be contacted. Members of the team went round to their houses, asking if they would be willing to come in at times that suited them. As they got closer to zero, it got more difficult. Patients couldn't be bothered to change, didn't want to, or simply objected to us badgering them. But as the team persisted, patients either said they didn't now want to come at all or agreed to come to one of the clinics that had been put on. So, astonishingly, the target was achieved. It was an incredible team effort, in tracking down patients, thinking of alternative pathways for booking and treating them, and acting so quickly.

- Relentless managers never give up.

- They go for targets: they go beyond targets.

- They are determined and focused.

- They are always dissatisfied and always curious.

- They have a direction but they steer rather than are driven.

- They keep reviewing where they are going.

- What they are doing develops. It is a personal narrative that makes sense to themselves, the main actor, and to those following the narrative.

- They see brick walls as challenges. They are prepared to go around them, and on occasion to back away from them to make progress.

My team were within days of the target deadline. They had got all patients who needed to be operated on booked in – except one. Team members contacted him, cajoled him, offered practically any time or date before the date that would suit him, but he said it simply didn't suit him and he would rather wait. In the normal sane, workaday world this would have been fine because this is what he wanted, but it would have breached the target with serious adverse consequences. The Medical Director offered to have a word with him. He said it would be very helpful to the hospital if the patient was able to come in before the deadline and asked if there was any chance of this. He also offered personally to operate upon the individual. The patient said, `Doctor, if it would be helpful, I would be happy to.' He was operated on hours before the deadline.

- They are pragmatic about actions. They are willing to try anything.

- They're respecters not breakers or avoiders of obligations and duties.

- They're honest (because honesty underpins and gives momentum to drive) at the same time as they are pushy.

- They are scouts and foragers. Their antennae are always up.

- They are extractors, miners, diggers for information, and for answers. They dig till they find what they are looking for.

- They are joiners, catalysts, creators of chain reactions.

- They are orchestrators, jugglers, balancers.

- They see one problem solved as the springboard to sorting out the next one: 'I've made a profit. How do I embed it? How do I increase it?' 'My school has achieved great exam results. How do I make sure that happens next year, and the year after and the year after that?'

## Steve Jobs

When the late Steve Jobs returned as CEO of Apple in the late 1990s because the company was in deep trouble, he realised that Apple computers were regarded as a sort of evolutionary dead end, ignored by the masses, looked down on by the experts and revered only by a small group of 'geeks', principally in publishing, design and architecture. He began to change that, initially by creating the iMac computer, which looked attractive – sexy, see-through and colourful. And so Apple computers began to gain broader appeal.

But Jobs also realised that simplicity, functionality and, above all, meeting people's most basic needs easily were what could give Apple an edge. With the iPod, Apple went to the front of the pack, creating a worldwide hit by meeting a simple, direct need of the everyman user. Next came the iPhone, then the iPad and so on and so forth. Apple has now become the universal purveyor of IT gizmos for us all. And it was all about relentlessness – starting from a difficult position, getting one thing right, then another, and then building on that, until finally the basic position has been turned round and there is a new platform for successfulness.

Relentlessness can bring connotations of pain and unpleasantness. To endure and thrive as a relentless manager, to really *be* one, you have to enjoy what you are doing, be animated by the effort and be enlarged by it. Because if you are not, then all those qualities outlined above will start to slip away and you will fail.

For me one of the best bellwethers of enjoyment is absorption in a task. We perform best when we are totally immersed, giving the task our all. This has been described by Mihaly Csikszentmihalyi in his classic book *Flow*. This absorption is quite different from forgetfulness, inattention and blinkeredness, all of which I discussed when describing the warning signs of failure. This type of absorption is about focus, about bringing all one has to bear on the task in hand. It is the essence, the apogee of relentless management.

# To sum up …

The way you achieve the opposite of failure, sustained successfulness as a manager, is by doing the following:

- adapting;

- using feedback;

- differentiating tasks and skills and then combining them to ensure delivery;

- internalising and using the five ideas;

- in particular, avoiding the delusive pursuit of perfection;

- instead, delivering and managing well but imperfectly.

In the following chapters, I will describe the skills needed and how to acquire them.

# 10

# The importance of being honest

A key point in my account of failure and specifically the fall into failure is the move from managing performance to managing perception, when delusion or deception set in. Tied up with this, and a key symptom of failure, is that communication itself dries up. That is because what is happening is not acknowledged or is being kept secret, as failure is revealed.

Happily, this analysis also brings with it two positive insights:

- Full, accurate and truthful communication is crucial in avoiding failure and ensuring good management.

- Worthwhile communication imparts a story, a narrative – it has something to say.

## The unbreakable triangle

Management which is functioning securely and vigilantly will have a **culture** which enables delivery, **systems** which are tested and which work, and **controls** which are comprehensive, alert, independent and objective. There has to be full two-way communication on these three key aspects of organisational wellbeing. The communication must include information, rules and narratives. I have put this insight together in a diagram, which I call 'the unbreakable triangle'.

The triangle illustrates the following principles:

- The mutual interaction between the three key components of organisations is crucial.

- Each component has two parts, one relating to what organisations and businesses *are*, the other to what you *do* to manage and make things happen in them.

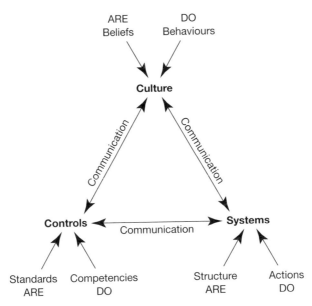

*The unbreakable triangle*

- Thus an organisation's culture is based upon beliefs (are) and behaviours (do), its systems on structures (are) and processes and actions (do), and its controls on standards (are) and competencies (do).

- The organisational unity it represents means ensuring that components interconnect and there is a full understanding of what is required of each in relation to the others. This means full communication between those aspects: two-way interaction with give and take, listening and speaking, a continual review and reassessment of what you and your business or organisation is and what you and it are actually doing.

- This unity provides stability.

If the links between any parts of the triangle are broken, if communication is disrupted, then an organisation will be heading for trouble; it won't know what it is doing wrong and it won't learn from it. If the triangle is working well, an organisation will be learning all the time, will realise when it has made mistakes and will do things better as and when it needs to.

In tackling failure, you restore communication first, thereby creating the outline of the triangle. Then you look at the three points of the triangle:

- culture: what you believe, how you behave;
- systems: creating structures, building processes, making things happen, tackling problems;
- controls: ensuring you have people with the necessary skills and that they are using them properly.

In finding out how things stand, test each aspect of the unbreakable triangle and test the interconnections and the communications between them. If aspects are not as they should be or if there is isolation between them, if the links are broken, then remedial action will be needed.

So what underlies all this? What is it that is so important?

# Honesty

It's all about **active honesty**. While it must be conceded that a plea for honesty is hardly earth-shattering, it cannot and should not be taken for granted and its meaning is not quite as obvious as it might seem at first sight.

- Honesty is the first and most fundamental building block in creating the opposite of failure.
- It is much more than simply telling the truth.
- It is about bringing clarity and transparency.
- In healthy managerial cultures, honesty is valued highly and drives managers to question and test performance, to admit problems and so open up the pathways to dealing with them.
- The unforgivable sin is not getting it wrong but failing to own up, and learn.
- Honesty brings order, good governance; its absence brings disorder, chaos.

- It requires consistent and continuous communication.

- The honest organisation learns, so this book says things that are in line with the notion of a learning organisation.

- However, honest organisations and honest behaviour in them are the prior and more defining characteristics, and understanding them is the key to much more than how organisations learn.

A manager has to be honest with him or herself and with others. It's the only way to ensure that perception and reality stay together. Honesty may mean making tough calls and saying, 'No, we can't afford that beautiful new sports hall even though it would be lovely for the local community, because it would bankrupt the council and send our community taxes shooting through the roof'; 'In order to meet targets we are compromising safety, so let's stop doing it'; 'That overseas venture was misconceived, it will never make a profit, let's get out of it.'

Real honesty – the honesty that all managers need to have in order to sustain success – is hard won and above all rooted in self-criticism. The honest manager understands that there is no such thing as getting everything right, however positive the performance and however benign the environment. Two questions always need to be asked: 'What are we doing wrong?' and 'How could we do better?' In an unhealthy organisation, these questions are not asked because the assumption is made that either everything is fine or that what is not fine is too difficult to change.

Problems fester because managers don't realise and/or don't own up to what is going wrong. The first antidote is to be clear about where you are having difficulty, where you and others are failing to move things forward. People often shy away from this and continue as if nothing is amiss, when they could be doing something to remedy matters. This means avoiding relying on 'comforting' explanations, such as why the problem is someone else's or why it will evaporate as quickly as it has appeared. So:

- Once you have identified that you have a serious problem, you must be honest about whether you can definitely fix it, whether you might be able to fix it or whether you do not believe you have the wherewithal to fix it.

- Assuming that you only *might* be able to fix it, you need to start preparing for alternative scenarios and seek help early to get you through these.

- If it is a problem you definitely don't think you can fix, then as early as possible you should seek whatever help it takes to provide you with the means, such as new skills or a change in the context, the circumstances, even the substance of what you are being asked to deliver.

# Passivity and fatalism

It is very important that, particularly in challenged situations, honesty doesn't lead to a sense of hopelessness and fatalism. 'We are doing what we are doing because we have no alternative, even though in our heart of hearts we don't believe it will or can work.' If that really is the case, then management should give up and pass the baton to someone else. This attitude is typically a symptom of slackness, of failing to see that there are alternatives and checking them out, a failure to be rigorously honest about what is going on and ploughing on regardless.

The mindsets are very important here. The dangerous and wrong mindset is one that sees confession of difficulty as a weakness which itself is to be avoided. The reverse is or should be true: namely, that confession of problems or in some cases failures is itself a means of clearing the ground to get at those problems. The most pernicious myth in management and much of human endeavour is that you can't make mistakes and you can't get away with them. We learn through our mistakes and by diagnosing what we did wrong, not by repeating them. Confession allows us to create a fault-tolerant organisation, which can see mistakes early and has a much better chance of dealing with them. Along with fault tolerance goes forgiveness. If people believe that their managers admit what they don't know then they feel free to admit it too. The problems that have been concealed come out of the woodwork and can then be dealt with.

A less passive but also mistaken and dangerous management approach is to notice but then ignore problems while they are still accumulating and causing damage. The rationale is 'These mistakes and problems are not central to what we are doing now. We will deal with them later.' In many cases you simply can't do this.

- Serious mistakes, wrong ways of doing things, won't stay as they are.

- They will pull effort further and further from the path it should be on.

- Correcting them early means correcting them simply.

## Toyota's lean production

This approach characterises the lean manufacturing process described by Womack and Jones in their epochal book *The Machine that Changed the World*. The book describes what Toyota's leaders saw when they came to learn about mass production in America just after the end of the Second World War. They observed a fast and in certain respects very efficient system, but one with an accumulation of mistakes on the production line. These were corrected at the end of the production line, at considerable expense and with great waste. What the Toyotans decided to do in setting up their version of mass production at Toyota – the approach which came to be known as lean production – was to deal with mistakes as they happened, correcting them while they and their consequences were small.

Such an approach is intrinsic to good management: grasping detail and acting early. This is not about losing focus; it is a cast of mind, an approach that underpins the focus that you have.

So what happens if you 'assume' or 'take for granted' instead of finding out? And how do you avoid that? When a national star rating system was introduced in the NHS, a whole range of organisations received poor ratings with a range of adverse effects – on reputation, on resourcing, and on the freedom to manage. This was despite the fact that they weren't in crisis or providing particularly bad services. What they had failed to do was to evaluate what it meant to meet the star rating criteria and take early, simple action to ensure they did. In many cases this would have been technical action, such as collecting data, processing it and passing it on; in other cases it meant administrative action such as commissioning and writing a report; and in other cases it meant taking very simple action to meet an easy objective. But in a perfectly real sense the lower assessment that these organisations got was deserved. They were not gauging the requirements that they now faced and that of itself was surely a reason for querying their capability.

One key aspect of active honesty is rigour. This involves defining in a particular instance what honesty involves – all of it, the full monty; probing to understand and persisting in your questioning until you have a clear and full picture:

- Why are our costs staying high but our sales declining?
- Can we really be providing quality work if we are getting such adverse feedback from our customers?
- The bottom-line figures are OK, but if we strip out the one-offs and special cases, are we really paying our way on a day-to-day basis?
- What happens when we run out of cash?

This sort of rigorous self-questioning is crucial in creating, understanding and reshaping the processes that we use in our work.

# Risk management and failure

If you are open and honest about the risks of failure occurring, you can make plans and contingencies to prevent it. To put it another way, become more aware of and better at using **risk management**. This is not about paper-based, box-ticking assessments. It is about mindsets and cultures, in which managers acknowledge real problems and difficulties. If you build this robustly into your approach, you will radically reduce the occasions in which you move from serious difficulty to catastrophic freefall. The alternative is not to manage the systems and processes that do exist but to become their servants and victims, as they mutate in response to whatever problem is currently experienced. The cost is enormous when that happens, so the prize is great.

However, as ever with management, insight must be followed by action. In May 2009, the *Financial Times* revealed that during a risk simulation planning exercise (described as secret 'war games') in 2004, bank regulators identified Northern Rock as the weak link in Britain's banking system, three years before Northern Rock's collapse, but did nothing as a result.

Risk management must lead to systematic comprehensive mapping of what is required for things to go right. It must then bring out each and every time where that pathway may change and cause things to start going wrong. Finally, it must lead you to plan what you will then do to correct things.

## Managing change at West Hertfordshire Hospitals

When I went to West Hertfordshire the key to 'saving' the organisation was seen as centralising acute hospital services in one place (Watford) rather than two (Watford and Hemel Hempstead). This was true. Centralisation was essential to create critical mass and safeguard viability, to ensure safety, to save resource and to guarantee adequate staffing. But it was an inherently complex and difficult project, described by the Chief Executive of the NHS, Sir David Nicholson, as the most demanding change facing any part of the NHS in that year.

I discovered that a hopelessly unrealistic, totally sketchy plan had been made to do this. Doctors were convinced there were too few beds and it couldn't work. A new building had been ordered, to be built offsite and put together Lego fashion, taking less than a year from beginning to end. Once handed over, it was to be prepared for use and opened in two weeks, with the simultaneous closure of Hemel Hempstead hospital. Any delay beyond this was assumed to be very costly. The adequacy of infrastructure services to cope with massively increased demands had not been explored.

In the light of the above, it was clear to me that carrying on exactly as planned would lead to disaster, as would leaving things as they were (which in any case was impossible at that stage). So this is what I did:

- The opening was delayed from late summer and a new date set, but only when we were confident it could be met.
- A winter opening was too risky so it was rescheduled for spring.
- Infrastructure services were investigated. In some cases, such as electricity supply, they were found to be woefully inadequate, but in the extra time now available this was put right.
- The alleged extra costs were investigated and ways found to mitigate nearly all of them.
- The unaffordable proposed 'wish list' of staffing proposals was torn up and an iterative process begun which related staffing needs to affordability. An affordable, safe staffing complement was achieved.
- A detailed timed plan for the transfer of services was prepared, spreading the transition over a much longer period and eliminating the need for any dangerous transfers.
- Doctors, nurses and others worked in taskforce groups to look at the right ways of working for the new, radically different circumstances and came up with methods of working which meant capacity would be sufficient.
- These were road tested by means of detailed, lifelike simulation events, and amended in the light of what happened there.
- Underpinning all this was a rigorous risk management plan, reviewed, checked and acted on constantly and publicly.

The change duly took place six months later than first intended. The transfer was flawless, with no patients encountering problems. The building was ready and fit for purpose; the infrastructure services all coped. The new service operated to budget, with sufficient staff. Because of better, faster diagnosis and treatment processes, patients were treated more quickly and didn't need to stay as long, so the reduction in beds was successful. Outcomes improved (fewer deaths and fewer recurrences of illness) and patient satisfaction also improved. Watford's rationalisation became a national model, and was described by the same Sir David Nicholson as a 'top drawer service'.

Every effort must be made to avoid the 'denial' phase of the failure process when perception and reality come apart. To stop people drifting into it, managers:

- need to become more 'fault tolerant';
- have to learn to be open about difficulties and blockages early on;
- should help their staff resolve them and not immediately move into blame;
- where (rarely) the resolution means bringing new hands to the job, they should help and support those being relieved of it, not just psychologically but materially.

# Understanding processes

Management is quintessentially about doing things and making things happen. Clarifying what we have to do is often the least of our problems. We spend most of our time on how we do this – and therein lie most of our difficulties. The 'how' of management really consists of two things:

- how to solve problems and understand the means to make the right things happen;
- how not just to put them in place once, but to ensure they stay in place and work permanently.

And what does making things work permanently mean? It means:

- smooth, uninterrupted flow;
- economy in the use of resources;
- the proper application of skills where they are needed;
- the elimination of diversions and detours in processes;
- the removal of empty intervals of waiting, both for those producing the end product, and for those receiving it.

## NARRATIVE

Conventionally, a narrative contains a beginning, a middle and an end, completed and joined by a passage through time. That's how you should look at processes and process design and redesign – as a story that needs to unfold, and that you can make unfold, coming to a desired end. But you need to be careful. You need to beware of ideal but unrealistic end points – fairy stories, which you can then fruitlessly try to arrange your work processes and resources to achieve – and of creating fictions. You can build your narratives around things which are not true, but if you do, the end product will also be false so your processes will do you no good.

Or you can – as you should – create processes which are true stories that accommodate your real circumstances and your realistic limitations and faults. They can then accommodate your realistic objectives and ambitions. This is the right way to look at processes, and it is very useful for all managers. Everyone relates to and lives stories, and stories are about lives. They bring processes alive. Processes, then, are *living*. They are a part of a business or organisation seen as an organism. Is it too fanciful to think of them as the skeleton, providing a framework for what managers do?

## EFFECTIVE PROCESSES

Effective processes take account of the multiple tasks that teams have in their work, and the multiple end products that have to be worked on simultaneously. The process for the producer or provider will be very different from the process for the end user or customer. To put it another way, good processes should provide good ends but they do not and cannot define them. At the most basic level, a process is there to meet an end user's requirement.

The end user typically wants something that works on time and only that. In the most straightforward cases, this is a product – a car, a house, a computer. In such cases, the process of producing is of no interest or relevance to the customer. This gets more complex as the end product and the user become interlinked as they do in the provision of a service, be it a meal in a restaurant, having one's hair done, watching a play or having a hip operation. Then the customer's, the consumer's, the patient's experience is part and parcel of the product.

In those cases, the processes that are used to deliver the end product are part of the end. But if we are to design processes properly, they must be distinguished.

A fatal mistake is to define the processes which form part of the customer experience, of satisfying the customer, and then assume that these are the processes which must be redesigned to get the best service delivery. What the customer wants is sometimes relatively standard but at other times it varies from customer to customer. When you go into a restaurant you are likely to want different food and drink from the person next to you; some people may want a quick meal and others a leisurely meal, and the way they want to be treated will differ but will be important to them.

If you start from the point of view of customer satisfaction, the processes the customer wants, then there will be too many processes, inefficiency and probably chaos. If, on the other hand, you understand the customer's requirements, you can create standard, efficient processes which you can then start to customise to meet their personal preferences, but without losing the necessary efficiency and workability.

# Redesigning to solve problems

Let's now examine problem solving as a process, drawing on the above analysis.

- You must have data (the necessary honesty) or you will have nothing to solve the problem with.

- If there are insufficient data, some will have to be produced.

- This could be achieved by using an existing but so far uninterpreted data set, or by collecting new data.

- You must move quickly to interrogate the data to see what and where the problem is.

- If the data collected don't yield answers then they are not sufficiently detailed or specific, and it will be necessary to dig deeper. The relevant data will be there somewhere.

- Most processes involve the passage of a significant amount of time and the key indicator of something going wrong is too much time being spent on them.

## Do or die

In Medway I set up a weekly meeting to go through all our key indicators. Where they were going out of line, those responsible had to offer an explanation, or, if they couldn't, find one by the next meeting, or sooner. They had to agree a series of actions to deal with the problem. These had to be based on understanding and improving the processes by which work was done. To emphasise its importance, the meeting was known as the 'Do or Die' meeting!

Those involved will start to build up an increasingly sophisticated picture of the flow of work:

- The method of mapping is less important than everyone involved understanding and being comfortable with whichever method is used.

- The most useful methodologies are those which identify key events, key decision points and the key information needed at particular times.

- Key decision points pinpoint blockages or queues. They will reveal the reason for the queue.

- Identified causes will throw up potential solutions.

- These need to be sifted for feasibility, acceptability, speed of application and cost.

- Some will make a difference, others not, but the net effect will be to increase performance.

- Each time a change is made, the effect will be to focus more on the residual problems.

- It is very rare for these problems to be complete brick walls. There is usually some chink in the wall, which if worked on hard and long enough from different angles creates a gap.

- It is equally important to work on the intervals where little is happening – the avoidable danger zones.

- They happen in administrative processes taking hours, days or weeks. Nothing is done until the last minute when all hell breaks loose. Usually what was done then could have been done much earlier.

- Drive back decision making to the earliest possible point, and identify barriers to keeping it there.

## Reducing waiting times at Medway

At Medway Hospital, waiting times were awful. Patients were being booked on to waiting lists in different ways by different secretaries and clerks acting on different instructions from different consultants, with chaotic results. Purposeful, informed behaviours by conscientious individuals to get individual patients their operating slot created inefficiency for the organisation as a whole, because each behaviour was unconnected and in competition with the next. So the staff frustrated each other and caused gridlock. Some patients were operated on after short waits; others were randomly selected for operation at any time; the remainder waited for the maximum allowable time before there was a huge scramble to get them operated on quickly.

By analysing what was going on and realising that it was our chosen processes that were at fault, we were able to develop a different approach. We mapped the effects of different styles of patient selection, good, bad and random, and the different-shaped waiting lists these produced. We unpicked them and created a simple, unified process to manage waiting lists based on using the processes which produced the 'good' shapes and avoiding those which produced the bad. We also worked through the changes in booking behaviour that would be necessary to effect this. We then taught our staff how to operate these new booking procedures. Finally, armed with a much more accurate assessment of both our actual and our required capacity, we were able to achieve much shorter waiting times.

Here's another example. Because mapping is applicable to the big and the small, using lean thinking process mapping we were able to reduce the wait for hearing aid tests from two years to two months, very quickly, and not by throwing resources at the problem. The issue was that we had a shortage of time for our ear, nose and throat (ENT) surgeons to see patients and approve them for hearing aids. Our first process mapping provided us with a solution: not the obvious one of getting more ENT surgeons, but using the highly skilled but not quite so pressurised audiologist in the same clinic to deal with some of the patients.

We authorised audiologists to order hearing aids directly in certain cases. We saw an immediate improvement, but it was not long lasting. A group of the audiologist's patients still needed to see the ENT surgeon and this group was now coming through faster because we had eliminated the first queue. We had simply created a second long queue.

This time we realised we had to alter the amount of resource at the bottleneck and identify which patients needed to go into which streams at the right times. That way we were able to match the availability of the audiologist and surgeon to patients by extending the role of the former and radically limiting the amount of ENT surgeon time that was necessary for the remaining small group. Result: we created process flow.

# To sum up …

- Process redesign is about means, not ends. But the ends must be clear from the outset.

- The ends will involve processes – the processes of consumer satisfaction – but these are different from, though sometimes related to, or similar to, the processes we design.

- Standardise first and customise second.

- Good process design is based on realism. With large numbers of customers, as we often have, we have a chance of getting it 95% right for 95% of our customers rather than 100% right for 10% of them. The 95/95 approach will allow us to push up to 96/96, 97/97, etc., whereas the 100/10 will lose us most of our customer base very quickly and the whole edifice will be in danger of tumbling down.

# 11

# Mining the data

For a body to remain healthy, its receptors and sensors need to be passing and receiving messages freely, speedily and accurately. So it is with a business. You have to know what's going on, so good management requires good information. And information is everywhere. It is the spindrift on the wind in the world in which we work, the plankton in the sea where we try to get things done. Steven Pinker in his book *How the Mind Works* says 'information itself is nothing special: it is found wherever causes leave effects. What is special is information processing.' Information will always be there. Equally, more information will always be available; more that may be useful or that you may not be able to cope with. What is certain is that there will always be enough information to give you some insight and to act upon if you process it and use it. For any business, any organisation, any project, any management task, this throws up a series of requirements.

## The devil is in the detail

- In 1999, NASA sent a probe to Mars. It was supposed to orbit and then land on the planet. But at the end of its descent, it crashed and was destroyed. The analysis of what went wrong showed one simple reason: someone working on the orbit and descent path had assumed the measurements were in metres. In fact they were in feet. Result: disaster. Billions of dollars and years of effort wasted.

- BAE was building a $2 billion dollar ultra-modern submarine, the HMS *Astute*, for the UK navy. When it was tested in December 2007, what one newspaper described as 'its most basic part', its oil pump, failed, causing huge damage, massive extra costs and major delays.

- On 15 December 2008, a headline in the London *Evening Standard* read: '£2 fuse brings £9 billion upgrade of West Coast [rail] line to a halt'.

- My last example is perhaps the most intriguing (and scary) of all. When the Large Hadron Collider at CERN in Geneva was being commissioned with the aim of finding the 'God' particle, the Higgs boson, it had to be shut down because the flow of particles was interfered with by a bird flying into the machine. This caused a six-month closedown to effect repairs at a cost of many millions, but one speculation had been that an interruption in the intended working of the machine might create a mini black hole in the space–time continuum, into which the whole earth might have been sucked. Small mistake, big consequence! Fortunately, the consequence didn't follow.

There is a widely held view that leadership and the role of senior management is about the bigger picture. In this chapter I will argue that this approach is fundamentally wrong. Understanding the smaller picture, if necessary the microscopic detail, is crucial to our understanding of the bigger picture, because otherwise the big picture will be the wrong picture. None of the disasters above would have happened had details not been overlooked. So:

- learn to love detail;
- attend to it, search it for what is significant;
- focus on that, use it to inform your understanding and actions;
- finally, use that significant detail to help shape your strategy.

# Finding the kernel of truth

Frequently, people tell you they don't have the information they need to manage an issue. They don't know what is going on and they can't. Never accept this. If people really were that ignorant, they wouldn't know there was a problem.

## MRSA

In a group of hospitals that were having big problems with the superbug MRSA, senior managers told me they couldn't do anything about the problem beyond what they were already doing. It was the sort of community where you got MRSA; it came into the hospital and they simply had to put up with it. They had no data to back this up but they firmly believed it. I asked for information on each service in their four different hospitals. These showed marked differences, for which there were a series of possible explanations, each more plausible than the last, and all suggesting that major improvement was possible. As a result, management was liberated to look at the real causes of the problem, real causes that it had some chance of fixing.

Many organisations and their managers have access to good information but they don't process it and use it to evaluate what is going on. In particular, they rely on overall figures. This is all right sometimes, but not generally. We need to be aware that we may be putting together essentially different things, apples and pears, which don't add up. Aggregation relies on averages even when the variations and differences are crucial. It's like having your head in the oven and your feet in the fridge, and saying that your average temperature is normal. Aggregation can be dangerously misleading. Split it and you will get to the kernel.

## Back trouble

A hospital having enormous problems with orthopaedic waiting lists had convinced itself that it didn't have enough capacity to reduce them and that therefore it needed a major increase in resources to do so.

On looking closely at its data, it was obvious there was a problem but it wasn't about resources. There were enough people, enough resources, enough time to deal with most patients presenting with most symptoms. The real problem was a small number of patients with very difficult back problems and only one person to treat them, with nowhere near enough time. Once that was understood, it was a matter of rejigging the balance of work to free up the time of the person with specialised skills and, when that still left a much smaller shortfall, farming out a very small number of patients to other centres which had those specialist skills and were prepared to take on the work at the right price.

Result: problem seen to be much smaller than thought, solution obvious, problem solved.

Having information available is a prerequisite to analysing it. Understanding what it means is one key to action. Another vital matter is *sharing it*. If information is communicated to those who can appreciate its meaning and significance, that in itself may be sufficient to create action.

During my time as CEO of Poole Hospital in the 1990s we extracted information about how each doctor used their time in outpatients, when they started, when they finished, how many patients they had seen, and so on. We shared this information generally – not only the individual's figures but the figures of the other doctors doing the same thing. This made a huge difference. In many cases people were unaware of exactly what they were or weren't doing. Simply seeing the information caused them to identify weaknesses and inefficiencies in their practice, which they readily eliminated. In other cases, seeing that colleagues were quicker or more productive led to competitive or shamed changes in behaviour. Where the difference persisted, it provided an opportunity for action with the individual that could be seen by others to be reasonable and fair.

### A case of competitive change

An outstanding neurosurgeon I knew told me how he had been keen to make his practice more efficient and save money. In common with his colleagues (as far as he knew), his patients stayed in hospital for 10 days after one operation he performed frequently. He felt there were bound to be all sorts of ways he could improve efficiency at the margins and reduce this, perhaps by 10%. He went along to an improvement session, hoping to learn how. A fellow surgeon spoke and explained how his patients stayed in for just four days after the operation in question. After recovering from the shock, my neurosurgeon friend realised that he could take a much more radical look at his practice than he had dreamed possible because someone else had done it successfully. Within a short time, his patients were staying in for only four days too.

# Approximating

You need to understand how accurate information needs to be. In some fields and at certain times, it needs to be totally accurate. To take the Large Hadron Collider again, an experiment in 2011 involving the most minutely precise measurements showed some particles travelled from Geneva to a location in Italy slightly faster than light can travel, which is impossible. Concern over this result was finally resolved when it wasn't repeated and the source of the apparent excess speed was found.

However, for most managers for most of the time, securing and using information is not about knowing everything perfectly. In the day-to-day managerial world, that sort of requirement would be a basic error and a recipe for paralysis.

Nor is it about knowing what's right overall, the aggregate answer, as I explained above. That conceals the vital importance of detail. What it is about is *approximate* truth. If you have searched, been through the detail and obtained a 'good enough' answer, an explanation which stands up, then act when you need to, go with it.

## Terminal 5, Heathrow

The fiasco of the opening of Terminal 5 at Heathrow Airport in March 2008 is informative.

The central problem was the loss of baggage. Volumes of baggage vary from hour to hour, day to day, plane to plane and passenger to passenger. These variations partly get smoothed out by statistical averaging, but also result in predictable peaks and troughs, for which capacity can be flexed and staffing altered. However, there was consistent evidence over a period of about a year that British Airways' baggage losses at Heathrow were among the worst in the industry worldwide, and not improving. Moreover, the training that had been undertaken looked to have ticked the boxes but in fact was inadequate: handlers didn't know what to do and security and baggage handling were working in opposite directions with no

▶

clear priority between them. BA seems to have assumed that technology would solve the problems, but the reality was that the system was simply not fit for purpose. Given all this, the disaster that happened was inevitable.

It could so easily have been avoided if BA had disaggregated the parts of the problem, mastered the detail and approximated. With approximation, you gather what information you can and act on it, even though it is partial and imperfect. Approximate information isn't once and for all: it is good enough information to get you going. Once you have better information, you can act again. Mastering detail and approximating would have enabled the system at Heathrow to be fixed before Terminal 5 was opened, and provided a system that would have worked well enough at the opening. That system could then have been refined and improved early on, without the breakdown that actually occurred.

# Using information for performance management

If the information isn't owned, if no one takes it as theirs or their responsibility, it can simply lie in the ether. In such circumstances, many pieces of information, even if they are vital, will not find a natural unequivocal owner. They may very well involve a whole lot of people, and a poor output or outcome may be ascribable to any one or a whole number of actions and actors.

## Performance management in practice

Poor performance often relates to a failure to meet demand and a linked lack of capacity. In a business I became involved with, people assumed they were managing sufficiently well, with the odd wobble. When things started to go wrong, the available information, which until then had been largely ignored, was seized upon by managers up and down the line, who each interpreted it from their own standpoint and set in hand action to put things right. The trouble was that it wasn't coordinated and it wasn't entirely consistent. So a number of responses happened at once, some of which replicated each other and some of which contradicted each other.

The way they got over it was simple: performance management. Each manager's responsibility to monitor what was going on was specified, and it was made clear what action it was their responsibility to take when action was needed. At each level they looked at the information needed, its regularity, the nature of the monitor and their responsibility, so that these never overlapped or duplicated, and no requisite action went unaccounted for. For the first time, the responsible operational manager knew exactly what was expected of him while the Chief Executive was also clear about the overall achievement and could signal when things were moving off track and required attention. As a result, the apparently chaotic capacity shortfall disappeared and management action became much swifter and more focused.

# Turning the world upside down

You have passed the first test, getting the information. You have passed the second test, questioning it, seeing what it means and trying to use it, but you are still stuck. Next try to turn the information round. Look at it through different filters. Here are two examples of what I mean.

## Crew management

In my current hospital, Great Ormond Street, a paediatric surgery team was looking for ways to reduce the time it took to affect the nine-minute handover of very vulnerable, very dependent patients immediately after an operation, from them to an intensive care unit (ICU) team. They were looking around

▶

for inspiration. Two doctors suggested that a great example of 'crew management' was in Formula 1 motor racing at pit stops, where both speed and absolute accuracy and reliability were of the essence. They contacted the McLaren and Ferrari teams (and aviation captains, people from another industry with something to offer) and persuaded them to work with them. The result was the development of a four-step procedure which halved information loss, reduced handover time by over a minute, and produced fewer technical errors.

When I arrived at West Herts, the government were using ethnic monitoring information to help eradicate any racial discrimination towards and between patients. It was judged a key yardstick of commitment and intent. No special efforts or measures had been taken to achieve it, on the grounds that many patients didn't want to reveal their ethnicity. In other places, with the right approach, combining sensitivity and persistence, and training all the front-line information-taking staff, it was being achieved, so it was clearly possible. I had brought a new discipline and rigour to target identification and achievement from the word 'go', so staff were now alert to the target's importance and the need to do everything possible to achieve it.

The problem was that we were now almost two-thirds of the way through the year with an achievement of 30% to date and a target for the year of 80%. Simple arithmetic showed that 100% achievement for the rest of the year wouldn't do it. Nonetheless we went for 100% and started to get near it, week by week. It was at that point that the lead Director realised something that everyone else had overlooked. Although most patients in the first seven months had been missed and although they were no longer our patients, their ethnic status hadn't changed and we could still contact them. So that's what we did. We set up a project and worked out detailed, systematic procedures which would reach all our former patients, using the new, effective techniques we had developed since my arrival. Week by week the percentages went up and by the year end we achieved over 80%. We achieved the impossible!

This story circulated round the hospital and beyond, and undoubtedly helped people to try new ideas and generate new solutions to problems that they would previously have given up on. This was now a place where (practically) anything was possible.

# To sum up ...

If you are vigilant, if you look for problems, then you will need useful information. But the usefulness of the information will in reality depend upon the use to which you put it. Time and again I have seen organisations and systems in difficulty which either didn't have information, and so *could* not manage, or didn't use the information they had, and so *did* not manage. It is crucial not only that information is gathered, but that how it can be used is thought through. So ask:

- How often is it necessary to check whether a particular process or output is on target?

- Who should do this?

- What action should be taken if it is off target?

- Are there systems that ensure this happens as a matter of course?

- Are those running the systems accountable for making these monitoring assessments and then acting if problems appear, if things go off track?

- Do they fully understand this?

- Is there a tight chain of information flow and response through the organisation from the delivery point to the most senior authority?

If these questions cannot be answered in the affirmative, and specifically, then the organisation is at unnecessary risk. On the other hand, if you have information and use it to manage performance in a regular way, then you will start to understand better the patterns you are seeing and the changes in them. It is vital to have or develop a mentality which sifts the detail that you gather for significance and highlights and checks something out of the ordinary to see if it is indeed significant or merely an aberration.

# 12

# Fault tolerance, randomness and pattern

In this chapter I will delve into what good, imperfect management means. It absolutely does not mean being satisfied too easily. It does mean striving hard to make the most of what you have, calibrating and reviewing and above all dealing credibly with the real world, a world in part always unknowable, ungraspable, unclear, unhelpful and chaotic.

## Living with imperfection

One of the great objectives of 21st-century engineering science is to create machines and computers which are 'fault tolerant'. This means that they are able to cope with mis-programming, defective instructions or circumstances that don't exactly fit the preordained bill. The key, though, is that having recognised the fault, the failure, the problem, or simply the new circumstance or environment, the machines do something about it, they adjust, they modify their approach.

Organic life has developed and evolved by becoming increasingly and, in ever more sophisticated ways, fault tolerant. Our bodies repair injuries and cope with a very adverse range of unexpected circumstances, and our consciousness is partly about re-computing the circumstances around us in all their adversity and unexpectedness and modifying our behaviours to accommodate them.

As for people, so for businesses. Think of it not as a matter of crude occasional correction but as always and constantly at the very heart – or in the genes – of an organisation. You want it to be hard-wired in: a subtle and complex process, endlessly adjusting and re-computing what it faces, and each time acting there and then on what it knows.

It is essential to emphasise that this approach is sharply differentiated from, indeed the converse of, slackness and simply allowing mistakes to accumulate. That is a completely different sort of tolerance: the process of inattention, of ploughing on regardless, which elsewhere in this book I categorise as the road to ruin. The process I am describing here is one where you acknowledge, identify and respond to failures, recognising they signal a new or altered problem which can then be coped with. It is quite different from tolerating mistakes *but* not learning from them, not amending actions as a result of them. That is the worst of both worlds.

Fault tolerance is necessary because the world outside is constantly changing. It will always defy our expectations and challenge our insights. Much of the future is unknown and some of it is perhaps unknowable. As you travel on, your horizon changes. The language you use, though, in these circumstances, tells you a lot about what you are seeing and how you are behaving. Four terms pop up again and again here: randomness, chance, inevitability and luck. They need to be treated with care because they easily become the excuse, the get-out clause. If it really is random or chance then the outcome is down to luck or inevitable. But is it?

# Managing the unknown

People have a tendency to characterise events that they can't explain as random or down to bad luck. This can imbue them with a sense of fatalism. But a willingness to confront the unknown, I argue in this chapter, is critical to successful management.

In fact, many apparently unexplained events have an underlying pattern and are, at least in part, predictable. The real world is one of imperfect data, partial understandings and chance discoveries. Most of the time people operate within the area of the known, while trying to cope with what is on the edge, and sometimes with the totally unknown. Donald Rumsfeld's originally much-derided but now universally quoted categorisation of situations into 'known knowns', 'known unknowns' and 'unknown unknowns' actually succinctly expresses this reality, although I would add a fourth one: 'unknown knowns' (what we think we know but actually don't).

There are always unknowns. They occur again and again in everyone's personal and working lives. Dealing with them is what life is all about and, for that reason, they are best seen not as barriers but as challenges and opportunities. Each area of unknown that is identified, understood and then managed moves across into the area of 'knowns'.

By contrast, what people don't realise they don't know – unknown unknowns – is a huge limit to their ability to fix things. Some of the most poignant examples of this come from schemes and organisations taking a leap forward in information, often in the form of shiny new IT schemes. NPfIT, the comprehensive multi-billion NHS IT investment programme covering the last several years was the largest IT investment in the world. It was implemented principally as a technical scheme. In fact, its potential for success lay not in how technically advanced it was but in how effectively it took into account the ways hospitals work and how doctors, nurses and patients behave. By not taking these basic factors into account – because those who managed it didn't realise they didn't know this – it went spectacularly wrong.

The manager's task is to find the pattern, whatever it is, and use it to reduce gradually the area of the unknown and the unmanageable. By breaking the problems down into small manageable bits, much of what appears to be random can be distilled into patterns based upon what people do, when, and what they need. There will always be a residue that is beyond anyone's control, but by reducing the 'unknown' substantially, management can increase its capacity to act, and then have a fresh go at what remains.

## London Transport

Not long ago, waits, difficulties and delays in accessing transport across London were perceived as inevitable because of variations in demand, necessary bottlenecks and the general unpredictability of problems. But London Transport showed that you could reduce queues and increase usage. It began with the underground system and straightforward things like simplifying fares to speed up payment, increasing capacity where it could and rationing (often by long ticket queues) where it couldn't. Automated ticketing helped, but the key innovation was probably the introduction of the Oyster card, which meant

▶

that people had an automatic, easily renewable way of travelling which avoided entry queues. Travellers were financially incentivised to use the cards, which further reduced queuing, and the system was extended to London buses, which in turn increased their popularity and encouraged cross-usage between different forms of transport. As the usage increased, other measures were taken to extend this easy on–easy off system, which is highly user friendly. Means were found to offer it to casual visitors, particularly tourists, and to extend it to the rail network within and around London. Bit by bit, travel across London by public transport became easier and more pleasant, with a positive outcome for the providers as well as their customers.

The 2012 London Olympics showed how good and how interconnected a system it has become, despite the ill-informed predictions of many Jeremiahs and Cassandras in the media of inevitable breakdown, meltdown and chaos. It coped with huge volumes and peak flows without waits or inconvenience.

# Turning randomness into patterns

Is something really random or does it just appear random to me because it hasn't been properly analysed? Some form of pattern, of coherence, underlies practically everything, and what people are often saying when they say that something is random is that they don't understand this pattern and because of that – or, possibly, anyway – it is outside their control. But until patterns are detected and made explicit, you cannot know what you can control and what you can't. Nor is an understanding that you can't control something the end of it. Once you know what you can't control, then you can start to develop avoidance strategies – contingencies that enable you to manage nonetheless.

## Reducing waiting times in emergency departments

Patients turning up at a hospital with an emergency problem have to be dealt with. That's why emergency departments exist. And one thing that is not at all unusual in them is a wait or a queue to be seen. This is true in the USA, in the UK, in Canada, in Sweden and no doubt in many other places around the world. The universality of these waits prompts many people to say that, unless you put enormous resources into solving this problem, then people will just have to wait because we can't predict who is coming in when. So when the UK government said that long waits in casualty were no longer acceptable and that all patients must be seen and treated within four hours, there was an outcry. It was impossible. I don't make this comment from a position of superiority. I was one of the hospital CEOs who said it!

But it was not all down to chance. A third of the patients only needed simple, straightforward treatment. So by setting up special units within emergency departments staffed by nurse practitioners to deal with 'minor injuries', 33% of the demand could be siphoned off. Next, there turned out to be predictable patterns depending on the day of the week or the time of day. The reason why many patients came in when they did was that a couple of hours earlier their GP had told them to. The likely timings of such interactions were highly predictable. So it was possible to amend staffing to reflect when more or fewer patients would be turning up at the door.

And so on. The random was reduced from 100% to 70% to 40% to 25% and lower. Countrywide over 95% of patients were now being seen within the 'impossible' four-hour target time.

The random had been turned into pattern and process. Word seeped out to the separately and differently run NHS systems in Scotland, Wales and Northern Ireland. They copied and they improved. Across Canada, where they had similar problems, they used the UK learning, and they improved too. So did Sweden and other countries.

So dealing with apparent randomness is about finding the pattern and the process within it and taking precautionary or preventive action. For those who don't, it's a matter of 'bad things always happen to me'. At the end of the famous film *The Big Sleep*, the beautiful blond turns to Bogart and says, 'Wish me luck, I got a raw deal.' In his unimpressed, laconic way, Bogart simply replies, 'Your kind always does.' Which kind are you?

Randomness transmutes into chance and chance transmutes into inevitability with surprising ease. Efforts to reduce infection from the superbug MRSA bring some of this out.

## Is MRSA inevitable?

There are huge variations in the prevalence of MRSA in hospitals in different countries, and in the UK it was relatively high. In Holland it is tiny, and in Denmark it is very low. The Dutch and the Danes don't think this is a matter of chance. They think it is a matter of their approach.

Even within English hospitals, there were huge variations in MRSA infections but the setting of a target reduction prompted cries of unfairness. It wasn't their fault. It was down to geography and social conditions. And because they assumed it was inevitable, they didn't make enormous efforts to avoid the things they could avoid. On the other hand, those who took the stance that things weren't inevitable and they could do things, behaved proactively and in a precautionary way, and their 'inevitable' MRSA infections reduced.

And what about chance? The famous scientist Louis Pasteur noted that 'Chance favours only the prepared mind.' If you don't know what is going on, you might well assume that no one does and no one can. You will almost certainly be wrong. Alternatively, you can start looking and keep looking, and you'll probably find something.

## Spikiness in MRSA infections

In visiting a whole range of hospitals that were trying to reduce their MRSA cases, I became used to looking at statistics based on small numbers. Typically the hospitals I visited would have had between zero and seven cases per month, so interpretation of variation required care. Very often people said, 'This peak [interestingly, it's usually a peak and not a trough]) was just random variation. There is nothing we can do about it and next month or the month after it's bound to be lower.' But – one of my recurring themes – this isn't necessarily so.

A hospital team noted that over the previous two years they had had peaks or spikes in the same two months. At first sight this seemed chance, but then they asked themselves if anything unusual went on in these two months. After much sifting and questioning, one event was peculiar to these four months but not to the other 20: twice a year, large numbers of junior medical staff moved on from their training posts and were replaced by newer, less experienced and, at that point, less well-trained staff. It was in their first month that the spikes occurred.

Their inference was that this was likely to be due to the pressure on new and inexperienced staff, the fact that what they needed to do to prevent infections hadn't been highlighted to them clearly enough and they hadn't fully absorbed it, with the result that they were likely to be making more mistakes, and engaging in less good practice. So the hospital at the next intake upped its emphasis in induction training on all aspects of infection prevention and control. The next time the figures came out for that month there was no spike; nor was there for the next changeover month. Having heard about this, we then found another hospital that had come to the same conclusion and had done the same thing with the same positive result.

Conclusion: This improvement is ready and waiting for everyone. Ascribing it to random variation means it's unlikely to be secured.

# Talent or luck?

Those of us who are not great sportsmen or sportswomen can all too easily assume that 'greatness' is a matter of being born with exceptional talents. But while this might have some part to play, people know in their heart of hearts that it's not entirely that way. Those who succeed may have natural talents but they have to try – and try very hard. Arnold Palmer, one of the greatest golfers of the twentieth century, gave his take on it: 'It's a funny thing. The more I practise, the luckier I get.' You need to practise at everything you do, to be relentless, obsessive even, never to give up, to get into that virtuous cycle of continuous improvement, recognising your imperfection but being restless with it.

And what about that strange and perhaps elusive commodity, luck? One of my favourite accounts of this is in the science fiction TV series *Red Dwarf*. In a particularly difficult situation and on a distant planet where the task is to unpick the most appallingly complex series of choices and make the right one, the protagonist discovers a series of positive viruses among which is a luck virus. If you become infected by it then you keep making lucky choices.

We know it isn't quite like that, but sometimes I think it isn't quite unlike it either. Napoleon was once asked why his generals were so lucky. He replied that he only appointed lucky generals. It's a funny, paradoxical comment and at first sight it seems only to say, 'I have great judgement in choosing the right sort of people with the right sort of attitude to make things happen.' And indeed that seems to be part of what he meant. But he went on to explain that when he was looking to choose a general, he went round the companies of his commanders, who were candidates to be new generals, and asked people what they thought of the candidates. When he was repeatedly told that a particular person was lucky, he appointed them. His reasoning was that people saw repeated success and, partly out of envy, partly out of disbelief, were reluctant to ascribe it to skills and judgement, although these were the real causes. Instead they ascribed it to luck.

## Dealing with bad luck

An organisation I was managing was recovering well from its previous failures. We were visited by a national inspection team and assumed they would see the improvement. When we received the report, we were shocked. It gave us the lowest possible markings on practically everything and painted a picture of an organisation that was getting almost nothing right. Our view was that the inspection team had come with an unconscious prior view that things must be bad and during their visit sought and found confirmatory evidence.

As we went through the report, we saw how it kept emphasising the worst of our failings and omissions without crediting us for the multitude of things we had done or were doing to make things better.

We were told that we had ten days in which to respond and that the response would have to be restricted to questioning matters of factual accuracy. We noted that the ten days included the Easter holiday. On the day we received the report, I called a meeting of all the people whose areas of responsibility were affected by the report. The chorus of response was loud and universal. It went something like this. 'This report simply isn't fair. What can we do to get the truth across?' I had also realised that, on the basis of the scores that we had been given, I would probably lose my job despite our other successes.

We went through the draft report point by point and when we felt a point was inaccurate or misleading we assigned individuals to marshal supporting evidence and rebut it. We created a small but highly dedicated team to coordinate this work and immediately start drafting our response. We met daily, assembling more and more detailed evidence that the statements and conclusions were not soundly based. We started to interlink themes and form a coherent narrative.

▶

We completed our response within the deadline and sent it with a dozen boxes of supporting documents. I sent a cover letter pointing out our concern at the amount of time we had had to raise questions on the report, and to assemble our case. I asked for personal assurances that all the work and supporting material we provided would be examined and considered. I asked the Director to monitor what was done with our response.

We heard nothing for two weeks, then we received a letter saying that we had sent so much material that they were not yet able to respond. Two weeks later we received a second response saying that it would be three months before we got a definitive response. Some months later we were given a revised upgraded marking that took us out of the bottom zone.

## To sum up ...

Maybe luck isn't that elusive. Maybe it's a matter of choice and persuasion and approach:

- You will get your share of good and bad luck. That isn't an excuse for inaction. Inaction will lead to failure.

- Disbelieve in the chance, the random, the unknowable, the unforeseeable.

- Seek out your luck, seek patterns, seek variations, seek explanations.

- When you get it, don't pause to say you are doing too well. Run with it.

- You will have earned it, you will need it and you can use it.

- That way the imperfect manager becomes the lucky manager, who becomes the successful manager.

# 13

# Gauging the environment

Much of this book and its prescriptions for management are about understanding, mastery and redesign of what is happening within a business or organisation. It is about the processes which deliver. But management cannot be restricted to this. It always operates within an external environment, within a context of possibilities and constraints, and these are typically in flux. They have a huge bearing on what is required to be successful and what has to be taken into account when doing so.

The most obvious example is the legal framework within which any business works and its requirement to make money rather than lose it, but it goes much further than this. In many situations, one business will be heavily dependent on another for its success because it is dependent on that business for the supply of essential goods or services, or because it depends on one business or buyer to want most of what it produces or provides. Other rule changes may fundamentally alter what is productive behaviour and what is likely to lead to problems, so for example in health care in England, we have moved from a block grant system of payment to one that relates payment to volume. Under the first system, survival often encouraged and indeed necessitated limiting work. Under the new system, the reverse is much more likely to be true. But a different stance is needed to respond properly to each. And the system never stands still. It shifts, it morphs, it subtly alters emphasis. You have to see that to understand it.

As so often is the case, what I am describing in this book is not unique to management but part of our everyday wider experience. It is relevant to marketing, but it goes much wider and much deeper. In terms of ideas, culture and politics, people often use terms such as 'the spirit of the age' or *zeitgeist*. Whatever we do in management there will be a zeitgeist, what people are expecting now, what is right for now, where the opportunities are now, and how they differ from the past. Sometimes a change in the zeitgeist is obvious, due to a fundamental change in regime or direction, or the circumstances in which everyone operates. You really have no excuse for not seeing this and responding to it. Sometimes it's subtler. Things change, what is fashionable alters, and so does what people admire and what they stop taking for granted. Managerially, you need to keep looking for this and asking yourself if it means that you need to change your behaviour or your actions – not to conform passively with it but to be in tune with it because it will impact upon what you have to do, what you have to achieve and what you can achieve.

# Horizon scanning

The tactic that the good manager should adopt is **horizon scanning**. This is what it involves:

- Scan what is coming up on the horizon.

- Weigh up everything you see there, not just the most obvious and most obviously relevant things there.

- Check out the things that may be significant.

- Evaluate whether each is a threat or an opportunity.

- Work out what you need either to defend yourself or take advantage of it.

- Ensure you understand the full implications before action is taken.

- But take action if what you discover warrants it.

- Be prepared to do so quickly, if you have to.

- Continually revisit the horizon and repeat the above as often as you need to.

## The case of hospital infections

In the last few years, dirty hospitals have become a big issue in the UK. The trouble is that it became an umbrella term for a lot of problems and it was also shorthand for a generalised concern about the increasing incidence of infections. The first natural response was to ensure that hospitals were clean, so many organisations did just that. Unfortunately, this didn't necessarily help with certain infections, such as the superbug MRSA, which is largely unaffected by a stricter general cleaning regime. Initially neither the public nor politicians realised this but they did notice that MRSA was getting worse, and this became an object of criticism. It proved a painful learning task for many hospitals to take on board a much more focused, rigorous and universal programme of MRSA reduction based principally on minimising the passing of infections via open-wound contact.

One of the early responses to the emergence of the MRSA superbug in many countries was to question the age-old process of screening and zero tolerance on the grounds that the bug was here to stay and that we had to live with it. In countries where zero tolerance approaches remained (e.g. Holland), MRSA remained largely absent. So horizon scanning is also about not letting your guard down too early, not changing a good practice until you are sure it is unnecessary.

As concern over infection mounted in the UK, attention shifted more towards *Clostridium difficile*, an infection with very little in common with MRSA, altogether more infectious and capable of resulting in a much higher death toll over a short period than MRSA. Managers who didn't understand the risks this infection posed and hadn't got their hospitals to take the specific preventative and eradication measures needed have run the risk of catastrophic outbreaks. There have been at least two such outbreaks causing deaths and leading to the removal of CEOs, executives and boards.

The lesson: You need to keep watching to see how things are changing around you, how risks are changing, notably what is deemed to be an acceptable or an unacceptable risk. That way you can keep walking the tightrope and avoid crashing down to disaster.

Many people would be of the opinion that George Bush was quite wrong when, at the end of the initial Iraq campaign in 2003, he told American troops on an aircraft carrier on the Arabian Gulf, 'mission accomplished'. Everyone now realises, including him, that this was far from being the case and has turned out to be a decade or so premature. For the most powerful man in the world and for the rest of us, it is necessary to ensure that our notion of what it is to succeed and to achieve a goal is the same as everyone else's.

# Rule changes

You must scan the horizon for rule changes which may affect your business and its ability to prosper. You don't need to be their victim even if they might and in some cases do cause catastrophic problems for some people. Here is a recipe for action:

1 Find out exactly what the rule changes are. The way they are presented second-hand is often not the way they are. Be sure you've got it before you decide on action.

2 At the same time, immediately start to assess how long you have to respond to the change that is affecting you.

3 Is the timing flexible and can you use that flexibility to your advantage?

4 Find out how absolute the coming rule change is and whether there is discretion in relation to any part of its application. How much discretion is there? Who has that discretion? Who has the power to change things?

5 What will dissuade, encourage or incentivise those people to exercise their power or discretion in your favour?

6 How can you soften the blow?

7 Where are you exposed? How can you fortify yourself or excise the exposed part?

8 How can you strengthen in the areas where you are strong so as to have spare capacity, and defend and buttress the areas where you are weak?

9 How can you use those parts of your organisation that are rock solid, unexposed and impregnable to protect you?

10 In normal circumstances, avoid at all costs an aggressive response. Unless it is so successful it knocks the threat right out, it is likely to reinforce the threat and bring it forward with hostility rather than neutrality.

11  When you are really cornered, a well-timed aggressive response can work, because it may show an agility and fleetness of foot that was not expected of you, but it will always have risks, as to some degree it will threaten others.

12  From the outset develop a plan B and beyond that consider at least the start of a plan C. You should work out and prepare your preferred plan of action fully and carefully. But it simply may not be possible to achieve it. At a certain point a step-by-step withdrawal could turn into a rout. It is vital you have one – or more – alternative scenario, even if it has to be a rather unpleasant one that you can always measure your preferred option against. And if things are really going wrong, at some point plan B will become preferable and will provide an escape hatch, a parachute. If you have no plan B, then your goose may be cooked.

13  Finally, the alternative plan must be realistic and implementable within the needed time frame. So it cannot just be an idle thought. It has to be robust and worked through, even though you hope never to have to use it. Some time ago, I reviewed the viability of a nationally and internationally famous hospital in need of fundamental capital investment. It was seeking nearly $2 billion worth of capital investment, requiring a tremendous leap of faith from government. When I asked what the organisation would do if it failed to get this investment, the response was 'We can't afford to fail. If we have an alternative we will show our weakness.' In my view they were wrong. People expect you to have an alternative, and if you don't then they are likely to have less sympathy for you.

# Togetherness and partnership

The environment is partly a product of weather and landscape, but your ability to live in it is determined at least as much by who else lives there, who you have to live with, your fellow inhabitants. This brings me on to the second part of what it means to gauge the environment.

In my experience, problems become very serious because they are not 'owned'. There is a process of passing the buck, transferring the responsibility of a growing problem to another organisation, thereby allowing the organisation which thinks it has passed the blame to carry on in a way which will almost certainly be contributing to the problem. I call this 'default-ual' decision making: in other words, don't make the decisions yourself and when they 'happen' hope the problem hasn't come in your direction.

I have seen major problems flare up in a number of cases, over a lack of sufficient finance in a system, a lack of agreement on what projects money should be invested in and a lack of consensus about what has to be done to achieve common targets. Where each organisation behaves to maximise its own benefit, it typically minimises the benefit it gives to every other organisation and overall substantially increases the problem. There is no recognition that there is, if you like, a managerial society where the overall benefit is important. There is no sense of 'civic' managerial duties and mutual responsibility, and in those circumstances problems typically snowball.

## The folly of assigning blame

Getting out of a problem collectively will probably mean leaving aside blame, so blame assignment must be seen as an expensive luxury and getting on with solving the problem as the priority. In one region I knew, a deficit had gradually grown: the money available to pay for healthcare was less than the money needed to provide it. Those organisations to which the problem was not directly attributable did not regard themselves as responsible and disowned it. Those who had the problem saw themselves dumped with a problem bigger than they could cope with and became paralysed into inactivity.

The right way forward is joint acceptance of the problem and a commitment to solve it in partnership, by whatever means are possible, rather than by some arbitrary notion of fairness or blame assignment which actually leaves the problem unresolved. In another area, the acute hospital had a serious financial problem deriving from over-optimistic, inattentive estimates of what its new hospital building would cost. Although many of those involved in the original agreements had left and the issue of personal blame was irrelevant, and although more money was clearly needed because the hospital could not be unbuilt and could only deliver a certain amount, people still continued to argue from incompatible positions. The result was that other problems got worse. In this situation buck-passing is possible for only so long. After a certain time the multiplying problems are a clear indictment of everyone.

And the solution? What emerges from the above examples is that, if a point can be reached such that responsibility is shared across organisations and problems are described as 'ours' rather than 'yours', then the insoluble becomes merely very difficult and the power of unified commitment starts to resolve the problem. Mechanisms which encourage and ensure this sharing, rather than allowing or even buttressing insular behaviour, are vital. They need to kick in very early on when any dangerous signals emerge.

The difficulties of insular behaviour don't simply occur at the early stages of challenge, prior to failure in an organisation or business. They are also a feature of organisations which are in the middle of failure. At their very lowest points, these organisations are seen as responsible for far more than they actually are. As discussed earlier in the book, they are seen as getting everything wrong. This over-reaction to their failure to see just what they were doing wrong has very negative consequences. Other organisations' response can also be destructive and create extra problems not just for the failed organisation but for its partners. So what are the lessons?

- When you are faced with insular behaviour you must use the leverage you have not to accept a partial, one-sided view or even a complete misrepresentation of the position. If you do accept it, recovery will probably not be possible.

- In doing this, you will use up some of the credit you have. This may be a problem if what is wrong in the rest of the system is not being tackled as well. Do it nonetheless.

- The space achieved has to be used to ensure improvement and to get 'buy-in' from other parties.

- Most difficult of all, the parties seeking to shift blame and responsibility must be persuaded to take on an element of it themselves. A failure on their part to accept responsibility is almost certain to lead to more general failure.

## To sum up ...

Good management isn't just about understanding and doing things within your business and your control. It's also about understanding, then reacting to, coping with and adapting to the whole environment in which you operate. That's the stuff right in front of you, your day-to-day interactions, partnerships, frustrations and difficulties. But it's also the stuff that shades away to the horizon and out of sight: government policies, changing legal requirements, changes to economic conditions and the economic outlook, and so on. If you deal with these, not only will it help you to avoid failure and to succeed in your own terms; it will also stop you getting drawn into the broadening failure I described in Chapter 3.

# 14

# The attentive manager

Good managers must develop a total alertness to what is going on, at every level: gauging the environment and weighing up what needs to be done. We've had a run of complaints here. Why? What is the common theme? What are we doing wrong? The **attentive manager** – and 'attentive' is a key word – will be continually choosing where to focus attention and where not to, when to reflect and when to act. Mastering detail is a crucial part of this.

Attention to detail and the big picture are not opposed: they must be aligned. It's all about scanning the horizon (Chapter 13) and examining the ground beneath our feet (Chapter 11). Only when we have done both will we see what has to be done and be ready to do it. Mastering both allows informed decision making and enables a manager to focus on what should be the organisation's highest priorities.

If, as I argued in Chapter 2, failure tends to come as a surprise and suddenly, the antidote is surely to do plenty of preparation, to look out for problems. This is very much more than working on instinct or gut feeling. With experienced managers, experienced people, that instinct is obviously going to be very helpful and is going to detect a certain number of problems. But in a complex, and even in a simple, organisation it won't detect them all. The system needs prompts; it needs good information.

Assumptions are sometimes necessary but it is important to remember that an assumption is only an assumption:

- Wherever you can, check out assumptions and replace them with factual detail. Go further than that: check everything you are taking for granted.

- If you have an assumption about what is happening, ask yourself what you need to demonstrate that it is true or untrue.

- If you can't make that observation directly, try and come at it from the side. There is usually someone somewhere who knows how to do that. There is usually some piece of information that offers you a way in.

- Try to find it and attend to what the information tells you.

- If it doesn't immediately support your assumption or if it seems a bit odd, don't discount it. It may be giving you a crucial pointer to something being off track.

- Once you have one suggestive piece of information, look for another and then another. They will either reinforce each other, setting you on the track to getting to the bottom of the problem, or they will reassure you, showing you that your assumption was right after all. This is a very useful thing to know.

If problems start to multiply, you are probably already at the eleventh hour. It will be very important in those circumstances to develop a proper sense of urgency and to focus relentlessly on understanding the linkage between the problems. If, once you have seen the linkage, the problems continue to multiply, if you don't know how to deal with them and you can't fully understand them, then it is your last chance to seek help and assistance before they overwhelm you.

# Dividing problems to tackle them

Problems often present themselves as large, generalised symptoms. This is outfacing and typically offers no clue to action. Don't get stuck there. The right thing to do at this stage is to try and divide what you see into what is all right or contextual and what is central to the issue you face. Keep on dividing and focusing time after time until not only are you clear, but the problem is of a manageable size. This may mean identifying successively a whole series of problems underlying the first perceived 'big' problem. Again, the methodology of lean thinking offers a useful way in. Look for the bottleneck, the blockage, the queue, and find out what is causing it. Ease the bottleneck or the queue and see if that solves the problem. If it merely leads to another bottleneck then go for that and so on.

This is attentive management, which contrasts with inattentive management. In difficult situations, one produces focus, the other panic. Time and again, organisations run into trouble because straightforward, but less than obvious issues are not dealt with. In Medway (before I arrived there), as the organisation sailed happily towards its new hospital, it did little to cope with worsening waiting lists and with setting up systems to stop them becoming worse, even though there were clear signals that this was important nationally. The view was taken, implicitly or explicitly, that as long as what those leading the organisation deemed important was achieved, namely delivering a new hospital, things would be OK. This proved to be a great error.

## Identify the main objective

The seemingly less obvious issues remain below the water level until, iceberg-like, they sink the *Titanic*. But, in reality, different objectives needn't be in competition. The most telling example of this that I have come across is when I was asked to survey several organisations which were in trouble as a result of their low star rating. To my surprise, it became apparent that many of them had failed to meet particular performance measures not because they were difficult – generally they were very easy – but because they had not understood them, had not attended to them or had not taken them seriously enough. Data had not been returned, the wrong data had been returned, or a report had not been written, leading to the automatic loss of a star.

# Being attentive

As I have already explained, a good manager needs to be attentive to the managerial, social and political environment in which he or she operates and be constantly scrutinising it, searching it and asking the question, 'Has anything changed that I now need to become alert to?'

Attentiveness is important. It means understanding the range of issues, seeing what is minor but could become major if neglected, and scanning with both a microscope and a telescope. It means, as the stone is thrown into the pool, watching not just the first ripple, but all the succeeding ripples. It is the managerial equivalent of a physicist trying to understand the universe. What happens in inconceivably large galaxies unimaginably large distances away and what happens to the Higgs boson subatomic particle on an unbelievably small scale and in an impossibly short time are both relevant.

Attentiveness goes even further. Attentive management means an alert business or organisation. An alert organisation will actually go 'scouting' for trouble and issues. This means seeking out issues which have the potential to be important, to prepare against their negative consequences and to get ahead so as to be able to jump quickly into a virtuous circle.

## Extending good practice

At Medway, once we had learnt how to manage waiting lists, we started to look further. We were enthusiastic and had become knowledgeable. We were keen to spread that knowledge and support our staff, and said so. A junior manager in X-ray came up with a proposal to extend the idea to booking in X-rays and other diagnostic imaging. At that time this had not been done anywhere else. We supported her and worked with her. It worked. Waiting times fell dramatically. This work then became a national exemplar.

# Elucidation

Often when you are trying to make a case, when you see the virtues of that case, others have a nasty habit of not necessarily getting it in the same way that you do, of not sharing your enthusiasm, of not giving priority to what you want them to give priority to. This can often be for the perfectly good reason that what you are suggesting does not merit priority, at least in others' eyes, or because your analysis is partial or flawed. But sometimes it's caused by your failure to get your case across well enough so that others can't help but see. In these circumstances, despite the fact that they have a good case, people often give up. They rightly see that merely repeating their arguments won't help, but is also likely to irritate and have other negative consequences as well as being a waste of their time.

But there is an alternative that should be considered: namely, to dig deeper, to seek other supporting explanations and presentations until the case is so obvious and compelling that everyone can see its force. Here's what happened to me at Medway Hospital.

## Relentless elucidation

The pressure on us was intense and even with lots of inventiveness and greater efficiency we were struggling. Not only was the emergency proportion of our work high (70/30 instead of 60/40), it was rising at four times the national average (i.e. over 10% instead of 3%).

I realised that an increase in emergencies of over 10% sounded high but in a harsh world was bearable. Then the light went on for me. The increase meant that emergency patients were no longer occupying 70% of our beds but over 77%. The really stunning insight came when I realised what had happened to the remaining beds. The available surgical capacity in one year had been reduced from 30% to under 23% of our beds (i.e. it had fallen by a quarter). That was definitely not bearable!

What was happening to us was taking away 25% of our capacity at a time when there was conclusive evidence that we needed more. To solve the problem we all had to recognise this, and do something about it. It was a long hard slog but after a full explanation and with supporting evidence, the resistance gradually dissolved and most people, whether providers or buyers of the service, agreed that more was needed. And so, because of that relentless elucidation, we achieved it.

# Restricting your priorities

The word 'priority' trips off the tongue very easily, and those who run governments or companies – or indeed any enterprise – are likely to use the term and need it. We can't do everything and we can't focus on everything, so it is important to make priorities.

When everything is a priority, nothing is a priority. It is therefore vital in any managed situation, but particularly challenged ones, that those who must act, and decide to what to devote their time to, have a sense both of what is bearing most heavily upon them, what matters most, and what they can impact on. They can then focus the finite amount of energy, skills and talents they have on those things and not on others.

I have already described in this book the fatal error of being driven by events and making everything a priority as a result, so that management moves from issue to issue without ever getting a grip, following through or securing proper solutions (see page 61). This also happens a great deal when priorities are externally imposed instead of internally assessed and chosen.

I have repeatedly seen organisations highlight ten or even twenty targets and then fail on all or nearly all of them, when a clear examination would have shown that only two or three of them were key. By devoting their prime attention to these key targets, they could have achieved them – at the expense of other, less important targets. By not devoting sufficient attention to them, neither the key nor other targets are achieved, which is the worst outcome of all.

Working in a large national corporation ultimately led by politicians, I have seen managers again and again asked to make very large numbers of goals 'priorities'. A few years ago someone added up the priorities for the NHS – specific, timed, deliverable priorities – and they came to more than 400. Merely to describe this is to show the futility of it. If over 400 goals are a priority then the truth is that nothing is a priority.

What is also interesting is that from time to time politicians or those with central oversight realise or get feedback (perhaps because their priorities are not being implemented) that they are simply setting too many. All too often they then make another error. Instead of eliminating large numbers of priorities or relegating them to lower status, they amalgamate them. I remember an instance where government officials issued fresh guidance in regard to healthcare saying that there were now only five or six priorities, which should make it much easier for managers on the ground. Unfortunately, if priority 1 is 'save the world', priority 2 is 'do everything perfectly' and priority 3 is 'ensure everyone lives forever' then we haven't got very far.

Allowing for some exaggeration, I hope the idea is clear. Real priorities must be specific enough to exclude as well as to include. They must lead us to specific courses of action and away from others, otherwise they are mere flannel.

Earlier in this book I outlined one of the most important warning signals of impending failure: namely, pursuit of a single obsessive and above all wrong objective. But singleness of focus isn't wrong in itself. The classic text showing the importance at a critical time of focusing on the right single objective is Eli Goldratt's *The Goal* with its approach called the Theory of Constraints. At times of crisis you may need to focus on one single goal. That is the limiting case. But more generally, the number of priorities needs to be small, typically five or fewer; they need to be ranked, because they will at times conflict with each other; and at any one time they need to exclude very large areas of potential activity. Let me give a very public example.

## A question of priorities

On Wednesday, 6 July 2005, the UK Prime Minister, Tony Blair, was interviewed in Singapore hours before he and the UK delegation made London's final bid presentation to the International Olympic Committee to stage the 2012 Games. The next day he was to fly to Gleneagles in Scotland to meet George Bush, Vladimir Putin and other world leaders at the G8 Summit that he was chairing to seek agreement to write off billions of dollars of African debt. A few days after that, with the UK holding the EU Presidency, he would have to chair a key meeting of the EU to come up with a compromise to resolve the deeply contentious multi-billion pound issue of Britain's EU rebate. He was asked about an issue that had just arisen in the UK, about people using cash or influence to get honours.

His response was very simple: 'I can't give you a view on that at the moment. My attention is currently entirely devoted to three things: getting the Olympics for London; making progress to help Africa at the G8 summit; and getting Britain's EU rebate sorted.' In the interview he didn't deviate from that. Within hours London had secured the Olympics for 2012, Blair caught a plane to Gleneagles where the G8 committed to invest $50 billion to fight poverty in Africa, and a few weeks later Britain's EU rebate was resolved.

But then, at 8.50 a.m. the following day, 7 July, three bombs exploded within 50 seconds of each other on three London

▶

underground trains and a fourth bomb exploded on a bus nearly an hour later; 52 commuters and 4 Islamic fundamentalist suicide bombers were killed, and 700 people were injured. Tony Blair left the G8 for London with only one priority, dealing with the aftermath and the consequences of that horrendous day.

# Understanding what is important

This leads us to the key to prioritising. It is about understanding that what is important in any organisation is a blend of its drives and its values, which will include excellent services and products, and a suitable environment for customers and staff. But it is also about gauging what is required of it externally from its customers, from its masters, from its stakeholders, how the weather is changing, what season it is. If the internal drive and the external requirements and constraints are balanced, the priorities will surface and they will be few indeed.

To prioritise is to deprioritise. It's a really acid test. As William Pitt the Younger, the British Prime Minister, said when he heard of Napoleon's key victories across Europe, 'Roll up that map [of Europe], it will not be wanted these ten years.' If you can't identity the things that are *not* important to you, then the truth is that you will dissipate your efforts and make them ineffectual, and you will fail.

The really important thing about priorities is that they alter and evolve. Sometimes, as Blair found, those priorities can change overnight; yesterday's priority may not be today's. Travelling around, experiencing organisations in trouble, one recurrent theme I have found is that they are still living out yesterday's priorities. Northern Rock went flat out for growth on the assumption that it could borrow cheap money to support this endlessly: even when it became impossible to do so, growth remained its priority. General Motors continued to rely on growth in the gas-guzzling end of the market, particularly SUVs, even though fuel shortages and growing concern over climate change rendered this strategy doomed. Napoleon put it very well: 'Plans are nothing, planning is everything.' So it is with priorities.

Prioritising means scanning the horizon and choosing what is important, turning the microscope on it, then grasping the issues and acting decisively and as quickly as you need. That doesn't mean hasty action, by the way. Decisiveness and prioritisation are different. I once came across a very decisive leader who loved nothing more than heading towards the metaphorical sound of gunfire. The trouble was that he could pick fights that weren't there and get into bigger fights than he could handle. As the approach had mixed success, it came to be characterised locally as 'ready, fire, aim'. It wasn't about prioritising.

So while prioritising, to be effective, does require decisiveness, it also needs deliberation, understanding, forethought. And it requires discrimination, not just at one but at many levels. It is hard enough to choose what your number one priority is; but that won't tell you how much attention and energy to give to it and of what sort. This is often an error made by those who love action. This is the priority; let's devote everything to it. Well, not necessarily. In order to take forward that priority in the right way, it may well not need all the resources and attention available, and there will be a price in relation to other major priorities and to the organisation as a whole if it takes resources and attention unnecessarily. So after determining your top priority, you then have to determine what attention to give it and how, and therefore what resources and attention to spare for the small number of other important priorities.

## The case of the superbug

The immediate reaction from the media, the public and politicians to news of the spread of the MRSA superbug in the UK was that if only more priority, more attention, more resources were given to this, the problem would be solved. This would have involved massive investment, making cleanliness in hospitals the ultimate goal, but it wouldn't have solved the problem. The key was not the attention *per se* but the proper focus of the attention. MRSA is not a very contagious bug, although it is a nasty one. What is crucial is not so much overall cleanliness as strict hygiene and decontamination procedures at the small number of critical incidences of exposure to the bug,

▶

principally where people have open wounds and there is contact with others. Once this is understood, it becomes clear that the general solution is about education, behaviour change and universal adoption of unambiguously safe procedures in critical circumstances. This requires a significant effort for a limited period from all staff, but the resource investment is small. So priority is the answer but it is crucial to define what the priority is, what it means and what lies behind it.

# To sum up …

- Hunt down causes not symptoms – both internal and external causes.

- Prioritise ruthlessly and deprioritise equally ruthlessly.

- Weigh up what is needed; and then accord that the priority in terms of the attention, the time and the resources it needs, but no more.

- At the end of the day, it is all about action.

- Good prioritisation serves to liberate appropriate action.

- Good prioritisation leads to action with a result, an execution culture rather than its hopeless opposite, a reactive, uninformed culture.

# 15

# Final thoughts

I have now described why failure happens, how to foresee it and how to avoid it. I have also described how to manage well, and the skills, behaviours and processes that are needed to do this in our uncertain world. But there are many intriguing questions left and I would like to finish the book by having a stab at a few of the questions that particularly intrigue me.

## Is success down to the individual or the approach?

When I tell people about my approach to management, one of the most frequently asked questions is: 'How much of the success of this is down to the approach and how much of it is down to the individual manager?' My answer is the obvious one: it's a combination of both. The late Steve Jobs was a great leader at Apple, a great innovator and a great reader of the environment. Jack Welch was a great 'doing' CEO at GE. Tiger Woods is a great golfer. Sir Alex Ferguson is a great football manager. Richard Branson is a great entrepreneur and innovator. Warren Buffett is a great investor. They are/were backed up by clearly thought-out approaches and considerable experience and learning, but they are/were also outstanding individuals. What even they haven't done is make all the right decisions, or get everything right. Steve Jobs made mistakes in sending Apple down an excluding route, Alex Ferguson has lost key matches and key titles, Richard Branson has pursued some enterprises and ideas that have turned out to be duds. Hey, they are living in the real world, they are imperfect. They are also exceptionally good at what they do. They have learnt from these things and moved on to other successes. All this explains why they are enduringly successful.

Anyone who realistically and honestly calibrates what they are capable of can do the same. Neither my approach nor theirs can make anyone 'great', but absorption, internalisation and use of the ideas in this book can and will improve their effectiveness, performance and satisfaction with the job and the task, because it will help to make sense of them, to give them order, to clarify goals and to show that achievement is indeed possible. And this is another positive learning I want to convey. Knowing your own and your approach's limits is the key to wisdom, success and successfulness. You will then get what you can out of them and yourself, but don't delude yourself that they can do more. Imperfect managers do things imperfectly but they get things done. They manage optimally, whereas perfect managers don't because they are a figment of the imagination.

This leads to a second set of key questions that people ask: 'How enduring is this approach? Can it be embedded so that it survives changes of personnel? If so, how?' Nothing is forever, but I believe that my approach can be hard-wired in and made a basic characteristic of any organisation's operation. It works and it lasts.

# Management or leadership?

The global edition of *The New York Times* of 28 April 2011 included a four-page advertising supplement prepared by *China Daily* of the People's Republic of China. Headlined 'Management Gap', it focused on 'the acute shortage of managers that is threatening the advance of its economy' and it began by referring to a recent report by management consultants, McKinsey & Co., highlighting that China needed four million middle managers, 3,000 senior managers and a further 100 managers capable of leading Global 500 companies if its corporate sector is to succeed. China has leaders and leadership, both good as far as I can tell, but it also needs managers to succeed. Managers are crucial to success. But why?

At the heart of my own experience and learning about management is an increasing realisation that management is about specifics rather than generalities. You need to focus on specifics, you learn from specifics, you do specific things and you implement specific solutions. You divide, you focus, you concentrate, to coin a phrase, to make things manageable.

My counter-learning has been to become wary, though not dismissive, of broader ideas, theories and concepts, theories that laud aggregate concepts, most noticeably leadership, but also wisdom, transformation and quantum leaps. Leadership is unspecific. It covers the whole world, such a variety of situations, circumstances and requirements that the generalisations all too often mean dilution to the point of meaninglessness. The leadership qualities of Winston Churchill in the Second World War, Shackleton bringing his men safely back from the Antarctic when the ship broke up, the captain of a successful football or other sporting team (or the manager), the head of a research team trying to develop a life-saving drug, the head of any business enterprise (massive variations there too) – they are all leaders, presumably all needing to show leadership. To set that out indicates that leadership is the wrong place to start. It's diffuse and indefinite and does not tell you what to do.

On the other hand, if you start with management requirements and tasks, you are likely to get onto something. The words I like, apart from those I have already mentioned, are do and do-ability, better, simpler, quicker, different. And look at the word 'manage' itself. Here is the dictionary definition, with comments, linking each part of the definition to what I have been saying in this book:

1 To bring about or succeed in accomplishing, sometimes despite difficulty or hardship [the whole subject of this book!]
2 To take charge or take care of [responsibility first, leadership second]
3 To dominate or influence a person by tact, flattery or artifice [influence rather than dominate, but communicate, communicate, communicate!]
4 To handle, direct, govern or control in action or use [make things happen]
5 To wield (a weapon, tool, etc.) [act, be a doer]

So that's what 'to manage' means. It's all about realism, coping, compromise, imperfection, but always anchored in achievement. 'I'll do what I can'. Stick with it!

# Managing to lead

In the summer of 2012 I was asked to comment on a thought-provoking interview with Sir Hugh Orde, formerly Chief Constable of Northern Ireland and President of the Association of Chief Police Officers. It raised for me the obvious question: 'How alike are the leadership and management challenges in healthcare and policing?' I had had to think hard about healthcare leadership challenges then, as I had just applied for and been offered the job of CEO at Great Ormond Street Hospital (GOSH) for Sick Children, and was now getting reactions to my departure from West Hertfordshire Hospital.

First, GOSH is an example (extreme perhaps) of the NHS truth that the brand is an awful lot bigger than the leader. The leader's role is about safeguarding and enhancing the brand; about quality, cohesiveness, competence and shared values; about being first among equals, a marshaller, enabler and catalyst. But you can only do that if you can make sense of the big picture and be a shaper of direction to match it. People want and expect you to understand the business. They are anxious that your expertise won't be full or specific enough because they are having to – and they want to – trust you. To be a good leader you have to show them you are a capable manager.

So what have I felt and experienced as a leaving leader? Guilt in response to expressions of warmth, gratefulness and concern because as a hospital CEO you really do belong to the organisation and are a vital cementer of it. This is because management in the NHS, and leadership even more so, is centrally pitched in human values and personal relationships and interactions. Any manager who wants to endure and be enduringly successful, let alone any leader, needs to attend to these, to want them and to be respectful of them.

At this point of transition for me, the importance of openness and transparency also struck me. On the one hand, it was cheering to be told that you had done what you said you would, and, on the other, chastening to see the question written across everyone's faces at GOSH, will you be who you say you are? Will you repay our trust?

Much that Sir Hugh Orde said about leading the police force aligned with my experience of being CEO of a large hospital, but two differences struck me: firstly, Sir Hugh's emphasis on literal bravery, a characteristic that we all admire but which is needed in metaphorical terms in my world, where it is about support, understanding and empathy; and secondly, the NHS and healthcare generally is a business of unsurpassed complexity (hospitals, according to management guru Peter Drucker are 'the most complex managed organisations in the world') where leadership involves understanding, blending and orchestrating the incredibly varied skills, intelligences and motivations of the most heterogeneous of workforces.

So there is much in common between a police force and a hospital, which is absolutely worth finding out about and understanding, but I am forced to conclude that I couldn't do Sir Hugh Orde's job and I don't think he could do mine. As for Sir Hugh and I, so I believe for most others. We can and should learn from each other. That way we both, we all, will do our jobs better. That's the basis on which I am offering my book.

# Good at being imperfect

Early on in this book I set out as one of its key guiding principles the fact that perfection is a delusion, likely to be the enemy not the friend; and also, very closely related to that, that there is no end point, that good management is about keeping going, about staying in the game. If that's so, ending this book with a wrap-up message is problematic. My way of dealing with it is to say that the wrap-up message is that there is no wrap-up message, that there is no perfection, that there is no end point and that the key to enduring success is continuation – more of the same.

But you can, and you must, learn lessons. The way forward is to consolidate and embed the ways of working, the ways of management that are described in this book. These are ways of working that recognise the inevitability of error and the importance of error and its recognition. They are about creating strategies based upon recognising your own imperfections; fault tolerance strategies that enable us to achieve.

# To sum up ...

What then is the advice for making vitality, if not permanent, at least long lasting? If there is no magic wand, then what is the next best thing? Here are some simple concluding ideas, admittedly mainly recaps:

1 Remember the sequence that this book describes and sets out.

- The sequence starts with imperfect.

- It moves through relentless choosing and prioritising.

- It communicates and shares and receives feedback as a result.

- This enables problem resolution or issue improvement.

- The communication and the sharing show achievements.

- They also highlight remaining or new errors, mistakes, problems and imperfections.

- Instead of seeing these as matters for despair, they are matters for positive attention, ground to work on, material for the next improvement and resolution.

- They are about keeping in this virtuous circle that we have got into, looping upwards and improving performance as we go around.

- This way the unbreakable triangle enables an unbroken and unbreaking cycle of improved performance.

2 Avoid complacency and never think you really have the solution: you won't have. Be a permanent watcher, and ensure you have tall watchtowers to look out from. Look inside for signs of overheating. Look widely: check and evaluate what others think, even if you don't accept what they say. Understanding why they say it and what is driving them will help you to respond better.

3 Remember the importance of contingencies. Always either have or be ready to flesh out a plan B. This is not necessarily about detail. It's about readiness to change direction, being geared up for something different.

4   Don't think you can create paradigm shifts, but look out for them happening, as they will, and often unexpectedly. Where these are radical enough:

- You may have to reposition or realign your whole effort.

- It is even possible that the shift will be such as to show you that your own task or your own contribution is over, that it may be time to hand over.

- It may be time for things to be done differently from the way you have done them.

If you foresee that, if you anticipate that change, then you can help your organisation, and you can certainly help yourself to move on smoothly to your own next challenge.

5   Search out luck. You can increase your chances of being lucky:

- Learn from, generalise each success.

- Do the converse: having found a failure and dealt with it, generalise your action by seeking out and eliminating anything like it elsewhere.

- Learn from others. Steal ideas shamelessly but critically.

- On the contrary, avoid the latest fad, the latest solution, the latest panacea, until you have evaluated just what it can and can't do for you.

- Keep asking yourself: what is the overriding metric? What is it here and now in the light of all I know, the priority, both in terms of what must be achieved and the time that must be given?

6   Think about the story you are experiencing, the story you are telling. Does it make sense? Does it look as though it will have a satisfactory ending? Think how you can shape one. Think about how the story won't actually have an end but will move on again.

7   … and don't panic!

# Appendix: A personal account

## 1. My world

This book is based on a sector I have worked in for many years and know well. Healthcare and in particular hospitals probably account for over 12% of global GDP. Just one hospital would constitute a major management undertaking. So what is a hospital? What goes on in it?

- It is a 24/7 organisation, dealing with the most important issues possible – illness and health, life and death. Its 'product' is the most complex of all, our bodies and our minds.

- It is a place of care and healing. We all believe in care and healing and know they are worthwhile. Hospitals and hospital staff run on a sense of altruism and a determination to 'do the right thing'.

- An average UK general hospital will serve a population of around a quarter of a million local residents. At least three-quarters of a million patients and visitors will pass through the hospital's doors every year. This figure is made up of 150,000 outpatients, 50,000 inpatients, 50,000 accident and emergency patients, 100,000 patients coming for tests, scans and examinations, and 50,000 coming in and out to do business with the 4,000 staff. Add to this a ratio of one visitor for every patient and you reach three-quarters of a million. In crude figures, on average everyone visits their hospital three times a year. Of course, some people visit it far more often and some don't visit it at all. But these figures show how important a part of the consciousness of the locality a hospital is.

- What sort of people come to this general hospital? More than half will be over 65. Hospitals are also places of beginnings and endings. Each year, perhaps 3,000 people will leave the hospital who didn't enter it because they were born there. Sadly, a significant number of people will go in but not leave because they die there.

- And what about the staff? They will all be under 65 and more of them will be in their 20s and 30s than in their 50s and 60s. And the vast majority of them, well over 80%, will be women. However, this may not be so apparent if you are dealing with managers or doctors, particular senior ones. There the gender split moves back to 50/50 or even in favour of a male majority. The point of emphasising this and the profile of patients is that the groups in question are from different segments of our society, are at different stages of their life and have different starting points and outlooks. To ensure they mix harmoniously and comprehendingly is therefore a crucial and complex matter.

- The range of professions and skills within a hospital is stunningly large. There is a village full of them – not just doctors and nurses, but maybe twenty or thirty recognised healthcare professions, such as pharmacists, physiotherapists, radiographers and biochemists. In places that have a hospital and a university, it is the hospital not the university that usually contains the largest number of staff with the highest level of qualifications.

- Hospital catering only achieves a high profile when someone doesn't like their food. It will be the biggest catering enterprise in its town or city. It will be serving nearly a million meals a year. Some will be incredibly specialised and it will be vital to the survival of the individual that they are right.

- People think of hospitals as large places dominating a large acreage, but as a physically closed world, a bit like a university campus. Visitors and staff often see them as bursting at the seams.

- There is another perspective. A typical hospital is a large car park with space for about 2,000 cars. Nestled among the cars and taking up perhaps 10% of the space available are the hospital buildings where care takes place. So hospitals usually find space to expand. But different parts of the hospital may be separated, which creates communication difficulties for patients and staff. And navigation for patients to find a place within a hospital can be a nightmare, particularly on their first visit. This is despite the fact that there will be an underlying logic to finding your way around the maze.

- From the point of view of space and time utilisation, the majority of space and much of the time is spent looking after inpatients. But for only a very small part of that time are patients being actively treated. Most of their stay is devoted to watchful waiting by staff, occasional intervention and to some degree simply queuing up for the next bit of activity. Active treatment will occupy a small percentage of the time, even if a patient is having an operation, which is clearly active treatment. If not, it will be much less.

- So viewed from this perspective, hospitals are large warehouses where patients are stored, hopefully in careful, attentive and sensitive ways. But how much of this 'storage' do they need? How much do they benefit from? Is the watchful waiting really helpful or is it time wasted, an unnecessary delay?

- Hospitals resemble nothing so much as a large repair shop, or series of repair shops. The aim isn't to create new, superior models and create a market for them, but to keep the ones already in circulation working well and as long as possible. Problem avoidance and problem prevention are at the heart of what a hospital does.

# 2. What happened to me at Medway

In 2001, the government introduced a star rating system for the NHS, up to three for the best performance and none for the worst. The word was that we would be a no-star Trust. Bad news! But because we were now known to be improving, notably on waiting lists, we were told we shouldn't feel too threatened. I was even asked if I would be willing to be involved in the national media coverage of the star ratings, on the grounds that this was a Trust that came out as a very poor performer but was already on the road to improvement. I agreed.

The BBC interviewer asked: 'What do you think about a star rating system that judges you to be amongst the worst?' I responded that I thought it was right and proper to evaluate performance in an objective way, though no system could be perfect. This system measured performance that was a year or more old and on a whole range of fronts we were now doing much, much better. The interview was friendly and the interviewer told me I had made a reasoned, reasonable case.

My next interview began in much the same way as the BBC interview and I responded along roughly the same lines. The journalist then said to me: 'Oh, you still believe that, even in the light of what the Secretary of State said about Medway and you in particular?' My head was starting to reel and I asked for an explanation. 'At the press conference he pointed out that there were 12 zero-rated Trusts, but amongst these, four had Chief Executives who had been in post for over 18 months and this put them into a particularly bad category. He said at the press conference that the Chief Executives of those Trusts would be given three months to substantially improve the performance of the Trust and if they did not they would be removed. Medway was one of the four.'

I realised the Secretary of State had decided to make this distinction and felt it had to be absolute. I fell just the wrong side of this line, having been in post just over 18 months as of that day, though less than 18 months at the end of the period being measured. I was told, 'We did what we could, but the Secretary of State was determined. We know your performance is improving and you'll be all right.' I knew this was sincere and meant well, but it was hardly reassuring. I put the phone down feeling like death warmed up. No one from any other local health organisation called to offer any sympathy or support, although one Chief Executive found time to tell the local paper that the zero rating was deserved.

I noted ruefully then and later that it was interesting that the Chief Executive of the NHS and his next-in-line at the Regional Office took the trouble personally to call and support me, whereas those in closer monitoring and partnering organisations didn't.

The next day I received calls giving their full support from the four local MPs. All said they would tell the Secretary of State the true position. News of the star rating had spread like wildfire around the hospital, particularly following my setting it out in a note to everyone, and for about three days I found myself stopped in the corridor every time I set foot on it. They were all supportive, all saying 'We are right with you, we know things are being sorted. It must be awful for you. Is there anything we can do?' Senior consultants, ward nursing staff and porters stopped me: everyone did. The local newspaper gave high prominence to the story and was sniffing round to find out how much substance there was in it. They interviewed me and other senior people but also put out feelers to members of our staff to see if they could get a counter-view. They couldn't.

The next day, as soon as the board assembled, our best-known non-executive, Prof. Bob Worcester, jumped in and said that in the light of the announcements of the star ratings he proposed a suspension of the normal order of business and further that the non-executives should immediately express a vote of confidence in the executive team and their actions to improve the hospital. Assuming this was then passed, the board should immediately notify the press, bring them in and read out the statement of support. It would then be in time for today's press coverage and become intrinsic to that coverage. That is exactly what happened. The press came in, the board response became part of a story that was neutral to positive, which was remarkable in the circumstances, and with that we gained the initiative.

Not only was I being stopped in the hospital by staff, but cards and letters started to pour in, mainly from staff, and there were also a couple of spontaneous demonstrations from patients to say they thought the rating was wrong. Most notably, all the patients in the day surgery unit insisted that their views be passed on to the press. The best card was one from all the staff in the Medical Admissions Unit, which simply said 'We think you are worth all these stars' and stuck on to it were a whole load of gold stars with the signatures of all the staff. It definitely helped!

A couple of days later I was idly leafing through the local daily and noticed that there was a leader from the editor about the hospital. This is what it said: 'I have been in Medway Hospital today with my son for an appointment. He was courteously and efficiently treated and we didn't have to wait. Walking around the hospital there was a positive buzz and I noticed that it was clean and tidy. It had lost that neglected look it used to have.'

'The star ratings seem to have got it wrong. Things really are changing in the NHS locally. I think there are two reasons. The first is that the government really is putting extra money into the NHS and it is beginning to show. The second is Jan Filochowski, he has definitely turned the hospital round ...' This was from the paper that would never allow anything good to be said about us less than two years before. That too was good!

After a day or two of all this I was running on a mixture of depression and elation and my tanks of adrenalin were close to empty. But deep inside I was hurt and to a degree angry.

Time passed. The welter of support had now diminished to a trickle. It was depressing. On the other hand, our already outstanding performance on waiting lists continued to improve further, so any question of a 'flash in the pan' could be easily discounted. The three months expired around Christmas, and still I had heard nothing about whether I would face summary dismissal at the end of it. Our performance continued to improve, and the previous nine months probably showed the best improvements in waiting lists of anywhere in the country (remember that our long waiting lists were the principal reason for our poor star rating).

The first Sunday in January, I went downstairs to take the papers out of the letterbox and started to flick through them on the kitchen table. I opened the *Sunday Times* first, read page 1 and turned to page 2, where a huge banner headline across the top of that page read 'Milburn to sack managers of failing hospitals'. It was a six-column article and as I read it my heart started to sink. The fate of one after another of the Chief Executives of the 'worst' no-star Trusts was described. In each case by some means or another they had been removed or were being removed from their posts. On and on the article went till I reached the bottom of the fifth column with no mention of Medway. My heart was thumping. Then I came across the following: 'but Ministers point to one startling exception, Medway, under the inspirational leadership of Jan Filochowski who is said to be responsible for some of the largest reductions in waiting lists, anywhere, ever'. It took a minute to sink in. I can't be sure, but I think I threw my arm in the air and went 'yes!'. I said to myself, 'I don't think you are going to be sacked.'

And so it proved. I received a letter from the NHS Chief Executive stating in a very low key way that it was felt that sufficient improvement had been made at Medway and I could keep my job.

# 3. My first experiences at Bath: wresting control of the problem

On my arrival at the Royal United Hospital, Bath, I took time to meet key people outside the Trust: monitors, funders, partners. There was lots of initial goodwill but it became evident very quickly that those outside felt under enormous pressure themselves and neither would nor could sit back and hope that my arrival would produce something. Many of them had moved into a very interventionist role and their instinct was not to move back from this until they were sure things were all right. The problem was that the intervention could only be superficially effective. It had disempowered and disenfranchised many of the key staff who were having trouble meeting waiting list and other targets. There was a strong atmosphere of fear in the organisation among those junior as well as senior staff who were bearing the brunt of this 'in your face' monitoring. I quickly sensed that externally people were looking at me to ensure my staff 'conformed' and delivered all the things that needed to be delivered by whatever means, however harsh and hard they might be. I knew from my experience at Medway that such an approach would not work. If you beat people hard enough, you don't make them compliant, you knock them senseless and eventually you kill them. We had to find another way.

This was borne in upon me very directly when I attended my first meeting of a Recovery Steering Group for the hospital, two weeks after my arrival. I was still learning the basics of the hospital and its problems and had no mastery of detail. The hospital had not put together the agenda, although it was all about the hospital. I realised that I was the only person from the hospital who had been invited. As we went through each item, those round the table turned to me for an answer. They wanted information, they wanted to know what was being done, and why things weren't being done, and then they wished to agree what was going to be done. I felt myself in an impossible position. I knew instinctively that this approach, if continued, would be destructive.

I sought to give myself and the hospital sufficient space actually to tackle the problems ourselves. In particular, I was astonished to be told that the hospital had to find £20 million savings and to be asked how I was going to do this. I knew that £20 million in a budget of £130 million was nearly impossible in any hospital in one year, but given that the Royal United was flat on its back, an utter impossibility in its case. The problem was that everyone else round the table knew it too but could not say so because that would have left a problem to be shared and dealt with more widely, and they were not ready to do that. So I simply said I did not accept the problems were necessarily as stated at that meeting and that I would want in due course to come back to them. My non-compliance and dissent from their collective view was deeply unpopular and resented. The group had to accept my right to do this as the newcomer, but I was using up valuable chips, which it would have been much better if I had not had to cash in at that point. I still feel I had to do that, however, and progressively over the next few months to shift the underlying perception of what was wrong from the damnable to the remediably bad.

When I left that meeting I resolved I would not be subjected to such a destructive and pointless session again. I ensured that I was unable to attend the next meeting, which happily was then called off as it was clearly going to be a case of Hamlet without the prince (or fall guy). I spoke to two key external monitors. I said I felt I could make progress, but they had to give me space and in particular to dismantle the team that was seeking to run the Trust by remote control, as it was having the effect of doing the opposite. I was promised this would be done and things eased up for a few weeks, but the leader of this effort did not believe holding back was the right thing to do and didn't believe in taking prisoners.

When I described my own difference of approach, I was told the person had been brought in to be hard and tough, and that was what was needed. I made it clear I disagreed fundamentally, and that if that approach persisted then I would be ending my secondment, as I did not believe I would be able to help resolve the problems. After much toing and froing, the team's role was ended and we were left to get on with the task of recovery. The external steering group was also disbanded. This took three months and consumed a great deal of energy and further credit with others.

I remain convinced that it was absolutely vital and that without it we would not have been able to achieve almost any of the things we did.

I was only able to do that because I was secure enough in my position to mean it when I threatened to walk away. But the effect of this removal of the shackles was enormous in the hospital, partly because people were learning how to solve their problems themselves, but also because it was the lifting of a yoke which they felt devalued and disempowered them, and treated them as inferiors. And internally, it massively helped my own credibility. I had got the tanks off our lawn! People realised they could trust me and that was crucial to moving on to more difficult problems.

# Index

# Read on

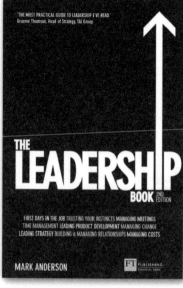

9780273776703

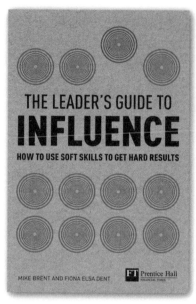

9780273729860

9780273751328

9780273776024

Available now online and at all good bookstores
**www.pearson-books.com**